EXPOSING THE **The Curse** ROOTS OF THE GENDER WAR

hair
le eyes texture porn rape the women doormat EYE CANDY exploitation depression
posed VS. women living in her... earth mirrors the painful
the bot...
plated
RESPEC... OBJECTIFICATION

Gary & Marie Wiens

Other books by Gary Wiens:

- *REACHING YOUR POWER POTENTIAL: Authority on Earth As It Is In Heaven*
- *BRIDAL INTERCESSION: Authority in Prayer Through Intimacy with Jesus*
- *COME TO PAPA: Encountering the Father Jesus Knew*

THE CURSE: Exposing The Roots Of The Gender War
Copyright © 2008
BHM Publishing
10017 133rd St. NW
Gig Harbor, WA 98329
www.burningheartministries.com

Printed in the United States of America
International Standard Book Number:

Table of Contents

Marie Wiens

Some years ago, when I was living in Seattle, I spoke with a friend named Peter Sheenstra, who was the Director of a counseling service in the Seattle area. Curious about his work in this field, I asked him what the most common symptoms of breakdown were in the marriages that he got involved with as a counselor. His reply came quickly and pointedly. He reported that the most common symptom was that the wife, frustrated and unfulfilled in the marriage, would start to nag her husband. She would begin to say things like "If only you would take more spiritual leadership in our home, if only you would pay more attention to me, if only you would help more with the kids, if only you would. . . (fill in the blank), then our marriage would be better." Please notice that these statements are *symptomatic* of the breakdown, not the cause of the breakdown. The answer is not merely for the woman to keep quiet; rather, other things must be set in place to prevent the frustration levels from becoming overwhelming. That is the point of this book, and we'll address some solutions later.

Peter went on to say that invariably the husband would

endure the nagging for awhile, and then respond by either silent withdrawal and isolation, or by rising up in anger and wounding the wife, either verbally, physically, or both. In either case, the fractures in the marriage relationship would be exposed, and the couple would eventually come to a crisis point.

I have for the most part enjoyed being a woman, but at the same time I have resented not being a man because of the privileges and honor that seem to go hand in hand with being male. As a business woman it seemed I was always struggling with being heard or being taken seriously. When I won the *Women of Enterprise* national entrepreneurial award in 1990 I found out that all of the other women who had won experienced the same difficulties. The issue of being a woman with leadership gifts in a man's world has been an ongoing point of tension in my life. Let me share a simple story that illustrates my point.

My husband Gary and I recently had a day off from our schedule of traveling and teaching, and we decided to take the time to play a round of golf at a nice public course in Kansas City. After finding the best price at *lastminutegolfer.com*, we found ourselves paired with two businessmen who were partners in a rapidly emerging business based in the area. They were delightful guys, kind and genial, and we had an enjoyable and even hilarious time, even though our quality of golfing left much to be desired. One thing, however, prodded a sensitive spot in my heart—the lack of regard for the presence and well-being of women that is typical of men in our culture. This lack of regard was expressed in a harmless way—the two men simply but repeatedly forgot that I was playing, and when the three guys were finished with their tee shots, these men jumped in their cart and forged ahead, forgetting that I was preparing to hit from the women's tees. More than half the time Gary had to whistle at them to wait for me to tee off, and they repeatedly apologized for their forgetfulness. Finally Gary remarked that they must not have many women working in their company, and they replied that they did indeed have lots of women employees. I could not help but wonder whether they regarded their female employees as valuable beyond the mere implications for the bottom line.

While the whole experience was certainly not damaging to me, it tweaked an issue in my heart that has been painful to me for some time. That issue is the place that women hold in the cultures of our day, and the negative attitudes in the hearts of men that are expressed in a variety of ways, ranging from simple indifference and disregard to outright rage and murderous hatred. For example, in much of the Church in America, it is rare to find a woman in leadership, or even to have a voice in what God might be saying to the Church.[1] In addition, in the secular culture the plight of women is increasingly horrific. Sex trafficking, the molestation of girls, rape and the physical abuse of women is rampant, and on the rise. Another telling statistic is the rise in the number of single moms raising their children alone because of divorce.

During the summer of 2006 I was in the prayer room at the International House of Prayer in Kansas City, crying out to the Lord regarding His women. I was in such a place of pain because the Holy Spirit was highlighting to me the abuse inflicted upon women and female children. I actually asked the Lord if He hated women, if He did not value the female gender as much as He did the male gender. I wondered about all the young girls that are being kidnapped and raped and those that are dying or being

---

[1] We understand the arguments that supposedly arise from biblical interpretation about this issue. However, those arguments are often selectively applied, and there is often a double standard when it comes to evaluating the qualifications of men in leadership.

beaten at the hands of men, in many cases their own fathers. I wept when I heard the current news report of a father in India who took his six-day-old twin baby girls and buried them alive so that he would not have to pay their dowries when they reached marrying age. He had been upset because he wanted a son, and instead got two daughters. So, he killed them in an unimaginably brutal way.

I also began to ask the Lord why women have such difficulty in the work place and why, apart from a few notable exceptions, they do not have much of a voice in the institutional Church. What are the reasons behind the brokenness that we see? Why are women patronized, marginalized, and brutalized the way they are, and why are men so constantly involved in such negative behavior toward women? The gender war, smoldering for centuries, has exploded into a full-blown firestorm, and I was determined to find the root system of it.

The Lord gave me the most stunning answer to my cry. The root causes behind these problems trace all the way back to the fall of mankind into sin, as recorded in Genesis 3. As we have begun to study and teach the things that you will read in this book, we have been amazed at the amount of understanding and healing that is coming to couples as well as singles.

The issue of the physical abuse of women is not the only thing that bothers me. I am continually dismayed by today's clothing styles that ignore any limits of modesty. Recently Gary and I were in Seattle teaching at a conference. We were having breakfast in a local restaurant when I noticed a teenaged girl in the booth ahead of us. Her clothing was so revealing that it was embarrassing for me. Later I noticed that many of the girls were dressed in tops that were startling even for my eyes. While watching the news in Seattle we noticed that much attention was being given

to the new trend in drive-thru coffee kiosks where female atten-
dants wear sexually provocative clothing. Sales have increased
significantly, apparently justifying the decision to dehumanize
these girls by making them fantasy objects rather than human
beings with any dignity. We've also seen that so many young boys
wear their pants so low that only their underwear covers them.
We continually wonder at the current state of things.

During that same time period we were listening to Dr. James
Dobson's show on radio. His guests were the All-Star baseball
player Albert Pujols and his wife Deidre. Deidre was explaining
that she travels with her husband most of the time as a protection for both of them. She went on to talk about the sexually ex-
plicit emails she receives directed at her husband and the scant-
ily-dressed girls that she sees at the baseball games. Dr. Dobson
acknowledged the change that has taken place in women today,
adding his observations on how they fight and curse like never
before. Although the program served to highlight this very issue
in a strong way, no practical solutions were offered to bring cor-
rection and resolution to the matter.

It seems to both Gary and me that women young and old are
desperate to find a sense of their own identity and destiny, but are
feeling an ever-increasing load of despair and heartsickness. The
noisy and brazen sounds coming from broken people like Rosie
O'Donnell are nothing more than cries from shattered little girls
longing for significance and power. It is as if something inside
them is saying, "Will someone notice me and think I am great
and beautiful?" It seems that, even in the face of a long history
of abuse and neglect, women are bent on getting man's approval
one way or the other even if it is destructive to their heart and
soul. The purpose of this book is to explore the reasons behind
these issues, and to propose some radical ideas that, if taken to

heart, will profoundly change the hearts of both men and women, and affect the status of women everywhere. We believe that the truths stated here—if embraced and acted upon—will result in a restoration of what God had in mind when He started the whole thing in the first place.

Our prayer is that you will read this book with a heart that is tuned to the heartbeat of our Father God, and to the mind of the Bridegroom, Jesus Christ. The good news the Bible brings us is that there is a way for us to achieve greatness in our lives. The Lord will not leave us alone in these struggles, but will send His Holy Spirit to show us the right way to grow in self-esteem and authority. What does He have in store for us as His people, and particularly for His women in the days and years to come, as we prepare for His return to the earth? May the Lord bless you as you search for His heart.

Marie Wiens
Seattle, Washington
April, 2008

CHAPTER ONE:

The Roots Of Human Devastation

One of the main things that we encounter as we travel and teach is the growing awareness of just how devastated so many people are, especially women, and especially in the arena of their identity. Or perhaps it is simply that, in a culture dominated by the male mindset, women find themselves with fewer options for masking their despair. One day Marie turned to me and asked "Why is it that women are so abused and tormented? Does God hate them? Did He create them to be less than men so they can be trampled on, used up, and thrown away?"

As a pastor and student of the Scriptures, I could easily come up with the correct biblical answer. The obvious answer to that cry is that God has created women out of love for His own glory, and therefore they are precious to Him. In my orientation of correct theology, I knew that through His sacrifice, Jesus had broken the power of the curse and made a way for both men and women to come to freedom. But Marie's cry was so deep and personally agonizing that I realized that the obvious answer would only sound trite and completely unfulfilling. If women really are precious to God, then why isn't our theology helping us all that much? Marie's questions were reinforced and amplified in a deep way. Why are we humans in such a mess?

We turned to the Scriptures, and as we sought the answers, we began to be filled with tremendous hope that there is a practical, real way that women and men can walk in the full freedom that Jesus purchased for us. The Holy Spirit spoke to Marie that the solution would be found in Genesis 3. We began to study and pray over the first three chapters of the Bible, and the Lord unveiled some interesting and powerful insights into how we have replaced God's original intent with a distorted method of obtaining our sense of identity and destiny. What we discovered has radically influenced our approach to dealing with these issues, both in our own lives, and in our dealings with other people. Please join us in our journey of discovery, so that you too might find the freedom God has in store for you!

What God Had In Mind

> *God spoke: "Let us make human beings in our image, make them reflecting our nature so they can be responsible for the fish in the sea, the birds in the air, the cattle, and, yes, Earth itself, and every animal that moves on the face of Earth." God created human beings; He created them godlike, reflecting God's nature. He created them male and female. God blessed them: "Prosper! Reproduce! Fill Earth! Take charge! Be responsible for fish in the sea and birds in the air, for every living thing that moves on the face of Earth." (Genesis 1:26-28, The Message)*

Adam and Eve were the first humans created by God. He gave them life so that in His perfect timing they would become full partners with Jesus in ruling the created universe.[1] They were unique creatures, formed by His own hand, and given life when God breathed His own Spirit into them. God wanted His life to be lived on the earth through these created people in the context of knowing His love. They were destined for immortality and for greatness, and were given limited authority for the purpose of training them for their destiny.

The Bible tells us in Genesis 2 that their lives were lived in perfect communion with God and with each other, pure and un-ashamed in complete transparency and trust, with all the necessary authority to govern and subdue the creation under God's leadership. The only prohibition in their lives was that they must not eat of the tree of the knowledge of good and evil, for if they disobeyed God's command, they would immediately experience separation from God, which is the essence of death. Here's how the Bible tells that part of the story:

> *God commanded the Man, "You can eat from any tree in the garden, except from the Tree-of-Knowledge-of-Good-and-Evil. Don't eat from it. The moment you eat from that tree, you're dead." (Genesis 2:16-17, The Message)*

Many have wondered why this temptation was placed in the Garden of Eden in the first place. If God wanted perfect people through whom He could express His life, why give them the opportunity to opt for an alternative? The answer is simply stated, but vast in its implications. God wanted *voluntary lovers*, not mere robots, and the only way to ensure voluntary love is with the presence of options. A relationship can only be called "love" when there is an option to choose love or to select a different course. God's blessings would be fully realized only for those who choose

---

1   See 2 Timothy 2:12; Revelation 20:6

to love Him as the first passion of their lives, instead of choosing to make a priority of the other options that are available. God's desire to have a people who would love Him passionately arises out of His own intense love. This love is so strong that the highest imagery He could give us to describe it is the love exhibited in family—that of a father for his children, and even greater, the love of a bridegroom for his bride. For example, in Psalm 103:13 we read this:

> *The Lord is like a father to His children, tender and compassionate to those who fear Him. (New Living Translation)*

Or consider this verse from Isaiah 62:5—

> *Your new name will be the City of God's Delight and the Bride of God, for the LORD delights in you and will claim you as his own. ...Then God will rejoice over you as a bridegroom rejoices over his bride. (New Living Translation)*

These verses help us to understand how passionately God loves His people who make up the Church, which is also called the Body of Christ.[2] He has given us the family unit, the marriage relationship, and the analogy of the human body to serve as windows into His character as the God who loves us and desires to be intimately involved with us in every dimension of our lives. It is no wonder that He cares passionately about the condition of marriages and families, because He intends that people who

---

2   We are defining "The Church" as the body of people throughout the world who have experienced God's forgiveness through the life, death, and resurrection of Jesus. They are those who have experienced regeneration by the power of the Holy Spirit, and are committed to following Jesus, becoming like Him as He leads them through this life into eternity.

don't know Him would look at Christian marriages and families and be able to see what God is really like.

Because of these and other Scriptures, the Bible refers to those who follow Jesus as "the Body of Christ," or more intimately as "the family of God." However, the highest and most intimate designation of God's people is "the Bride of Christ."

The Right Posture of Responding to God

So, in the Garden of Eden, the man and the woman stood side by side, partners comparable to and suitable for one another under the direction of the Father. They were before the Father, gazing at Him, listening to Him, gaining their sense of identity and destiny from Him, and receiving from His hand all that they needed for their daily existence. Now, I'm going to say something that is very important for you as the reader to understand: *Both man and woman were created to stand in a humble posture of listening to the Father's voice, receiving everything from Him as the normal course of their lives. In this way, both man and woman gave expression to the feminine, or receptive side of human nature.* This receptive attitude was best modeled by Jesus Himself, who stated that on His own He could do nothing, but that everything He did happened in response to the voice and activity of His Father, God.[3] Isaiah prophesied about Jesus' posture of listening when he wrote:

> *The Master, God, has given me a well-taught tongue, so I know how to encourage tired people. He wakes me up in the morning, wakes me up, opens my ears to listen as one ready to take orders. The Master, God, opened my ears, and I didn't go back to sleep. (Isaiah 50:4-5a, The Message)*

3   See John 5:19-20

Out of the humility of receiving everything from the Father, Jesus then could stand in His masculine authority and declare powerful things like *"Let there be light!"* or *"Your faith has made you well,"* and *"Lazarus, come forth!"* In the same way, Adam and Eve were to stand in humility, receptive before the Father, hearing His voice, and then exercising their masculine authority as His partners under His leadership. This is the plan of God to give dignity and tremendous authority to human beings—to hear the voice of God, enjoy Him in a relationship of intimacy, and then stand in that delegated authority and rule the very creation as His sons and daughters. This is not about being robotic slaves to an almighty tyrant—this is about understanding that, in God's mind, authority and power were delegated to humans, and were meant to be exercised in the context of intimacy and love.

A friend of ours, Julie Meyer, is a singer and worship leader at the International House of Prayer in Kansas City, better known as IHOP-KC. She also has a strong prophetic gift, which means that she hears the voice of the Lord speaking something to her, and then she speaks it, and then it happens! In March of 2007, we were having an unseasonably warm spell of weather, and it seemed as though winter had moved directly into summer, and was skipping springtime! Our trees all produced buds and new leaves, and Marie bought a lot of flowers for the gardens around our home. Then one day, Julie got up in a meeting at the House of Prayer and declared that the Lord had spoken to her through a dream. She spoke strongly, asserting that we should not put away our winter clothes, that there was coming a harsh cold spell complete with a snowstorm that had a particular spiritual meaning for all of us. It seemed like a far-fetched thing to say at the time, because the weather was so nice it seemed impossible that it would snow again that season.

Well, on the first weekend of April, after we planted all our flowers, the cold spell and snowstorm happened. We had the coldest Easter Sunday on record in Kansas City, and what Julie said literally came true. How did this happen? Did Julie have control over the weather? Yes, to an extent she did, because she heard the voice of the Lord and declared it to the rest of us. She listened from a feminine posture, and then she spoke with masculine authority, and what she said happened because it came from the place of listening and obeying.

This is how we humans were meant to live—listening to God, receiving from Him as the earth receives a seed planted in it. Then we speak with His authority over the things that concern us, and that seed brings forth its fruit. But when we turn away from Him and listen to other voices, we lose our authority and inherit trouble instead. God created us to desire Him, and to find all our joy in His presence and provision.

An Interesting Complication

Now it's important to notice one interesting complication to this whole matter: the commandment about the forbidden tree was given to the man *before* the creation of the woman. She didn't yet exist when God told the man not to eat of that tree. God left it to the man to communicate this important restriction to his wife. And from what we will see as we go through the story, he did just that, and perhaps more.

So, the central issue confronting the newly created humans was one of love. Would they value the desire and will of their Creator over their own interests? Would they trust Him to bring fullness to their lives in due time, or would they choose their own way, attempting to realize their destiny apart from His will? Their relationship with God, and the success of their relationship with each other, was completely dependent upon the choices they would make over this issue.

How The Trouble Began

Here's what the Bible says about what happened that started all the trouble in the first place:

> *The serpent was clever, more clever than any wild animal God had made. He spoke to the Woman: "Do I understand that God told you not to eat from any tree in the garden?" The Woman said to the serpent, "Not at all. We can eat from the trees in the garden. It's only about the tree in the middle of the garden that God said, 'Don't eat from it; don't even touch it or you'll die.'" The serpent told the Woman, "You won't die. God knows that the moment you eat from that tree, you'll see what's really going on. You'll be just like God, knowing everything, ranging all the way from good to evil." When the Woman saw that the tree looked like good eating and realized what she would get out of it—she'd know everything!—she took and ate the fruit and then gave some to her husband, and he ate. (Genesis 3:1-6, The Message)*

Do you notice anything different in this section from what God told Adam in the first place? It's in the response that Eve gave to the serpent. Satan's question was, "Did God tell you not to eat of any tree in the garden?" Now, notice how Eve exaggerated God's commandment. She said, "No, we can eat from any tree except the one in the center of the garden. God said, 'Don't eat from that one, and don't even touch it, or you will die.'"

How did she get to that second part about not touching the fruit? I imagine that it might have happened something like this: Adam and Eve were walking about the garden one day, and they came near that tree. Eve saw the fruit of it, and it looked very tasty, so she began to go near it. I can imagine Adam getting real nervous and saying, "Eve, don't eat that fruit! God said if we eat that fruit we'll die!" Then in her sweet and gorgeous innocence, perhaps Eve responded, "But Adam, honey, it looks so-o-o good!" And Adam might have said, "Eve, darling, God was really serious about this, so please don't go there; as a matter of fact, *don't even touch it!* I was alone for a long time, and I want you around, so just stay away from that tree!"

The Real Temptation

It is so important to see that when Satan came to tempt them, *the temptation was not focused on their desire for greatness*. The certainty of greatness had been promised to them. God created male and female in His own image, and gave them an amazing set of privileges as stewards over the earth in response to God's leadership. Notice that in Genesis 1:28 this blessing was spoken to both of them, not just to the man. This assignment was to train them for their eternal destiny as partners with Jesus in ruling the universe.

The next thing that is important to see is that their desire for pleasure was not wrong. God created us for maximum pleasure! Psalm 16:11 states that *"in Your presence is fullness of joy, and at Your right hand are pleasures forevermore!"* The issue here was not that the first humans desired to experience pleasure.

We must also see that their sin was not their desire to be like God. The Bible tells us that it is our destiny as believers in Jesus to be like Him, perfectly corresponding to Him as His Bride, just like Eve was the perfect counterpart to Adam. 1 John 3:2 says *"But friends, that's exactly who we are: children of God. And that's only the beginning. Who knows how we'll end up! What we know is that when Christ is openly revealed, we'll see him— and in seeing him, become like him."* When Jesus returns and we see Him face to face, we shall be transformed into His likeness and His promises will be realized.

Becoming like God was the destiny of those first humans, and it is our destiny as well. It was a promise rooted in God's desire for a bride for His Son, not a grandiose dream for little creatures who should have known better.

So, we see that Satan was not tempting them with something outside their reach. We are not tempted by things that have no point of connection in our hearts. The only temptations that hook us are those that resonate with our inborn sense of dignity, significance, and destiny. These are the temptations that grab our attention and cause us to lose our focus. Even the most perverted form of pleasure-seeking is rooted in the inner God-given knowledge that He has created us for joy rather than despair, for exhilaration rather than boredom. No, Satan was not tempting them with pleasure or greatness; rather, *he tempted them with a shortcut*, with the promise that if they would take charge of their own destiny by eating the fruit, *they could have their destiny now, on their terms*. By grabbing the forbidden fruit, they thought they could be like God on their timetable instead of waiting for His.

Adam and Eve were tempted to take their eyes off of God and focus on a created thing as the source of their identity, destiny, and hope. You see, God never intended created things—people, places, possessions, positions—to be the *source* of our joy, of our identity and dignity. These things are only the vehicles of His blessing, and nothing more. Our attention should always be fixed on Him and on His agenda. Matthew 6:32-33 says it so simply and clearly:

> *What I'm trying to do here is to get you to relax, to not be so preoccupied with getting, so you can respond to God's giving. People who don't know God and the way he works fuss over these things, but you know both God and how he works. Steep your life in God-reality, God-initiative, God-provisions. Don't worry about missing out. You'll find all your everyday human concerns will be met. (The Message)*

When we try to make created things—money, people and their opinions, job status, social standing, etc.—the source of our identity and destiny, we are in for big trouble, but not because God doesn't want those things for us. He simply wants us to desire *Him* first, to love Him with everything in us, and then He will give us all those other things in His perfect timing. Again, we love Him by spending time with Him in worship and prayer, by learning to understand His ways and His will, and by living in obedience to what we understand. One great expression of this is to learn how to pray over one another by agreeing with what God's Word declares about us.[4]

In the great tragedy of Genesis 3, Adam and Eve took their eyes off of God, turned their ears from His voice, and listened to the distorted promises of the enemy. He told them that eating the fruit would make them wise, that the created thing had the power to give them what had been promised them, on their terms and timetable. They looked away from their true Source,

---

4   See the sample prayer that I pray over Marie every day. It's located on page 87-88.

and bent themselves toward the creature, trusting a created thing to give them what only the Creator could give them. When this happened, God was forced to pronounce a judgment upon the serpent and on the people, a series of curses that plague us to this day. In the next chapter we'll take a look at what God was forced to speak over Satan and over the woman, a curse which has resulted in the horrible abuse and misuse of women and children since that day.

CHAPTER TWO:

The Judgment on the Woman

God gives His commands to His children out of love and out of a desire to bless them beyond their wildest dreams. His commands are designed to lead us into the fullness of His goodness. So, when there is clear revelation about what God wants us to do, it is essential to follow that revelation and obey the word of the Lord. To fail in this means that we will have to face the disciplinary judgments of God. Again, His disciplines are motivated by love, and the Scripture affirms that, like the good Father He is, God corrects His children.[1] Because Adam and Eve were in a perfect relationship with God and heard His commands clearly, they were living in an unspoiled expression of what God created them to be.[2] However, because of the level of intimacy they had with God, they were also highly accountable to obey the things God had told them to do and not to do. So, when they sinned, the judgment was swift and terrible. Notice the horrifying statement that God makes to Satan in the aftermath of his interference with the woman:

1 See Hebrews 12:5-8
2 See Genesis 1:26-31; also Genesis 2:15-25

I'm declaring war between you and the Woman, between your offspring and hers. He'll wound your head, you'll wound His heel. (Genesis 3:15b, The Message)

What a terrifying word this is! God declared a war between Satan and the Woman that will continue until Satan is fully crushed and defeated! It's no wonder such terror and trouble comes to women. Satan is at war with them under the judgment of God, until the seed of the woman—Jesus—crushes the head of Satan himself. This is why women are the focus of Satan's rage and hatred, and why he goes to such lengths to bring disgrace and ruin to their gender.

Here's a key point: Jesus has *already* crushed the head of Satan through His death and resurrection. Therefore, for those who know Jesus and trust Him with their lives, *there is no need to continue to be trapped in the penalty of God's judgment.* We can begin *now* to live in the blessings of God that will be fully released when Jesus returns to the earth to set up His literal Kingdom. By coming to know Jesus intimately, and by living as He taught us to live, we can begin to know the freedom that He intended us to have from the beginning. When we gain understanding of God's truth concerning us, we can begin to act and make decisions that make sense and benefit our lives.

Let's consider more closely what God said to the woman, and then we'll look at the judgment on the man in the next chapter.

To the woman He said: "I will greatly multiply your sorrow and your conception; in pain you shall bring forth children; your desire shall be for your husband, and he shall rule over you." (Genesis 3:16, NKJV)

God's judgment was that the woman would experience

multiplied pain in all areas of life, especially in childbirth, and that she would be dependent upon men to define her and give her significance. The war between Satan and the woman would result in terrible difficulty, multiplied pain and sorrows in her life. On top of that, more and greater trouble comes in the last two phrases: *"Your desire shall be for your husband, and he shall rule over you."*

Here's why the impact of these words is so devastating: the word for *"desire"* in the Hebrew language implies obsession, a desire *"bordering on disease."*[3] This desire would take the shape of a violent craving, a total distortion of what God intended human desire to be. In other words, from that point on, the woman would look to man in a diseased way, specifically to her husband but generally to men in authority, for her identity, destiny, and sense of significance.[4] It is as though God said, *"Since you wanted to look sideways to the created fruit for what you can only get from Me, let that be your judgment. You will obsessively look to man, specifically your husband, for what he cannot give you, and it will cause you great pain and sorrow."*

This obsession is accompanied by great fear in the heart of the woman. She fixes her hope on the man, yet instinctively knows that he cannot provide what only God can give her, and so she lives in the grip of a constant, underlying fear that she will not be recognized or fulfilled.

Some good friends of ours experienced this dynamic of fear some years ago as they faced a particular business decision. Mark had come across an investment opportunity related to their busi-

3   From Keil & Delitzsch Commentary on the Old Testament: New Updated Edition, Electronic Database. Copyright (c) 1996 by Hendrickson Publishers, Inc.

4   This issue has direct implications for men as well, which we will address in the next chapter.

ness that really seemed right to him. It had a measure of risk, to be sure, but their assets were sufficient for the situation. Kathy, however, was caught in a web of fear that the cost of the investment was too high, and would spell their doom. Even though Mark had the facts to back him up, Kathy was riddled with anxiety over the decision. Her irrational emotions of fear were so great that she couldn't see the situation with objective eyes.

The story turns out well. Mark was gracious in the situation, and decided to postpone the decision until Kathy felt more at peace. The window of opportunity eventually closed, but Mark continued to pray and ask God to make it happen in the right time. Finally, the situation presented itself again, and this time Kathy was ready to trust God and take the risk. She turned her eyes to the Lord instead of to her husband, and the result has been phenomenal. The investment has paid off in a spectacular fashion, and both Mark and Kathy have learned that God will honor and reward those who look to Him instead of to one another for security.

The word *"desire"* also carries the implication of manipulative control. In her diseased desire woman finds ways to manipulate the man to give her what she wants, even though the attempts are doomed from the start. God will not allow Himself to be replaced in our lives. If we try to get from some other source what we can only get from Him, we will inevitably be frustrated to the point of great pain. It is this obsessive desire for recognition and approval that drives the woman to unholy strategies, including sensuality, using her femininity for power and control. Yet it never achieves for her what she wants, only bringing further trouble and pain. So, in that pain, the woman uses controlling methods—food, spending, fantasy, alcohol, sex, or inappropriate clothing to gain attention or comfort.

Marie and I were recently talking with our son David Shinners, who is an executive with Blue Cross/Blue Shield in the Seattle area. He works as a trainer and team coach within the executive structure of this organization, and was telling us about the difficulties working with certain women in his office. His assessment, not from a spiritual perspective but from a purely practical standpoint as a leader, was that the women he works with are constantly manipulating situations to further their own interests and advancement.

Not only do women use political manipulation to further their interests, they can also become adept at using sensuality as a weapon of control. I cannot think of a better example of this in our time than the pathetic and tragic figure of Paris Hilton, the heiress to the Hilton Hotel fortune. Here is a pretty young girl who has all the resources of an earthly inheritance, and yet she has been obsessed with manipulating the media and everyone else around her to give her the attention she craves. Her act is simply a scream for someone to tell her that she is significant and that her life has meaning. During the spring and early summer of 2007, while she was in jail for defying her probation on a drunk driving charge, she suddenly declared that she found God, and He told her to "quit acting dumb." I hope this was a legitimate encounter, and that someone who is truly godly will follow up with her and lead her into the destiny for which God created her.

Another example of this manipulation for power was in the news recently. A physically beautiful 23-year old woman was prohibited from boarding an airplane because the clothes she was wearing were too revealing. While we applaud the willingness of the airline to uphold some measure of a standard of morality, we are grieved at the need for it. Because of the publicity generated by the encounter, the young woman was contacted by *Playboy* magazine for a photo spread, including being featured on the cover. When she was asked about her reasons for agreeing to the exposure, she replied that exhibiting her body gave her a feeling of power and control over men. By doing this, she could manipulate them into giving her what she craves—a sense of affirmation and power. What she does not realize is that she is being systematically destroyed by an enemy who wants her to lose all control and all hope of reaching the destiny for which God created her.

God's judgment on the woman did not stop there. The next part of His judgment statement is just as chilling: *"He (the husband, or man) will rule over you."* This "ruling" is not the kind of leadership and authority that God had in mind when He created the humans. It is a "lording over," a tyrannical kind of rule that diminishes both man and woman, and consigns the woman to the level of property and servant. God made the woman to be a suitable helper to her husband, not merely a housekeeper, servant, or a convenient means of sexual release. But under the terms of the judgment, the man will relate to the woman in a broken way, resulting in much dissatisfaction and pain. The man who does not live by the Holy Spirit's leadership has only two ways of reacting to the woman's desire. On the one hand he can acquiesce and give in to her demands, or on the other he can rise up in anger and abuse his position of authority. Deep inside his heart, he knows that he does not have what she wants, that he is inadequate to meet her needs, and so he reacts by silencing her, by avoiding her, or by abusing her. This reality is reflected in the statistic that one of every four girls will be sexually abused by her father or some other male that she knows.

Man also rules over a woman by forcing her to become "one of the boys" in order to have any point of impact in his life. When

Marie was making her fortune in the food industry in the 1980s, men made room for her, not because she was a woman to be valued in her own right, but because she had a product they wanted that would be profitable for them. In order to survive in that world, Marie was forced to become almost masculine, to enforce her will by power and positional authority. As far as she was allowed to, she became "one of the boys," and gained a place of influence because of the excellence of her product. One situation illustrates the tension of this: the guys that worked for Marie developed a football pool based on predicting the scores of National Football League games. Even though Marie was the president of the company, the men did not want to allow her to participate in the pool. Finally, after much persuasion, she was permitted to play. Marie went to her sons, got a lot of great advice, and eventually won all the money in the pool. For just a brief moment, she became "one of the guys," but she found it to be a temporary status.

My point is this: even though Marie was highly competent at what she did, there were doors in that "man's world" that were closed to her, simply because she is a woman. One production foreman refused to allow her into his production plant because no women were allowed there, even though she was the president of the company! His distorted masculinity was so threatened by her presence that he had to rise up and "rule over her" to whatever degree he could, and so he kept her out of his space. Marie had to send her male business partner to finalize the transaction.

Another situation occurred when Marie was working as a fundraiser for a Christian missionary organization. A number of the men who were her peers in the job setting liked to play golf. Marie also likes to play golf, and plays well enough to merit being included in the occasional game. However, she was never invited to join the group, and so one day she asked a co-worker why. His reply was something like this: "Marie, when we go play golf, we want to scratch and spit and pass gas, and we just don't want you around when we do that!"

At one point, driven by the desire to find acceptance among her peers in the business world, Marie bought a beautiful red Harley-Davidson motorcycle. She got all the accessories—the leather riding clothes, boots, gloves—and went for a 700-mile cross-country ride with the guys. She became a bit of a legend among the guys because, although she was very inexperienced, she endured the journey to the end. Though it was a legitimate and exhilarating adventure, in the long term even that did not satisfy her longing to belong and establish her identity. We have been created for something more than that.

As Marie and I study these things and talk together about what the Holy Spirit is showing us, she always agonizes about the horrifying situations in which many women find themselves trapped. We hear endless stories of marriages that are in desperate trouble, not to mention reports of the abuse, rape and murder of little girls, the sorrow and difficulty of women, whether it be in the work place or at the hands of men, and the young female adults suffering from sexually transmitted diseases. Many times we have heard men say horrible things about women, as was in evidence on a recent "Oprah" show. The topic of discussion, which aroused anger and sadness in all who heard it, was the violent and abusive words used to describe women in contemporary media, specifically the rap music culture. We have also heard husbands refer to their wives as "low or high maintenance," as though the value placed on a woman is inversely proportional to her "maintenance level." If she doesn't disrupt the man's life, doesn't interfere with his goals or priorities, and provides good sex, good food and a clean house, then she is "low maintenance" and therefore more valuable than a wife whose needs and desires are more pronounced. However, the Holy Spirit touched my heart recently with this understanding: the ministry of Jesus *is* to a high-maintenance Bride! I am high-maintenance! Jesus is constantly listening to me, constantly available to me, and His concern for me is constant and beyond my understanding. The Bride that He values is worthy of all His attention and affection.

As Marie and I travel extensively in the ministry of teaching and healing, we repeatedly find the women of the Church, including the wives of pastors and leaders, to be in lots of trouble. Many are angry, and feel hopeless at every level of their lives. They are often overweight, often battling depression and loneliness, and often oppressed by such conditions as fibromyalgia and chronic fatigue syndrome. Many women feel that the place they hold in their husbands' lives is low on the totem pole of priorities. Work or ministry comes first (for many leaders in the Church, ministry equals God), recreational pursuits come in second, and the wives feel as though they are tacked on some place after that. They feel insignificant and that their opinions don't matter. They have little or nothing to offer to the man's world they live in, so they focus on the kids and begin to suffer the effects of low self-esteem, loneliness, fear, and depression. Is it any wonder that a horrible television show like *"Desperate Housewives"* is a highly-rated segment of their week? Is it any wonder that prescriptions for anti-depressants are at an all-time high?

Because Eve chose to listen to the enemy instead of to God, she reaped this great trouble. Through her sin she brought increased sorrow upon herself and the women who would follow her. In her pride Eve gratified herself, thinking she could be powerful and have privileges *apart from listening to God, apart from His will and timing.* She wanted masculine authority without feminine humility. Instead of waiting for Him to release the fullness of His perfect plan, Eve refused to be content with her feminine nature. She seized the place of authority, and opened the door for grief, pain, and fear to be visited upon the women of the earth. It was this sin that brought millions of tears into the female experience and showers of trouble and sorrows upon them. Honoring the dignity of choice He gave the woman, God removed His hand of protection and blessing, thereby multiplying all human sorrows and troubles.

Despite overwhelming evidence to the contrary, there is an answer and a solution to all this sorrow and pain. Whether you are married or single—for the issues of persecution and pain plague single and married women alike—as you continue to read, you will discover how to be released from the chains that bind you. But first, let's look at the results of this judgment in the lives of women.

The Effects Of The Curse Are Everywhere!

The brutalization of women has been rampant in human culture all through history, and it is no different in our era. The statistics on sex trafficking are too horrific to digest, and even modern cultures carry on age-old traditions of abuse, particularly sexual abuse. Consider, for example, this paragraph from Dr. Emily Chong's study on women in the context of the Korean-American church:

> The history of Korean women has been the incessant process of devaluing women in order to view them as dehumanized objects or puppets. In traditional society (1890-1910), the home was a virtual prison; women were

not even permitted to eat a bowl of gruel, or were condemned to an etiquette that required a minimal display
of emotion—even to their children, as only a smile was
allowed (S. K. Jung 1995:6). Such a period in history for
Korean women can be summarized as an era of *han* (*han*
is a unique Korean concept of unresolved sorrow, grief,
and regret) and tears. A Korean proverb interprets this
grief, "If a woman's heart fills with *han*, there will be
frost even in summer." This oppressive quality of life was
a breath full of *han* for women, when loss of human rights
through gender discrimination was socially acceptable.[5]

In a personal conversation in Seoul, Korea, in September of
2007, Dr. Chong told Marie and me that, well into the 20th cen-
tury, it was common for a Korean man to have two or three mis-
tresses living in the home together with his wife and children.
As Western values entered the culture, this practice is no longer
common, but the infidelity has not disappeared. Now the mis-
tresses are kept in apartments, and according to Dr. Chong, every
night in Korea there are some 300,000 visits to prostitutes in a
nation of 45 million people. This is but one cultural example of
unthinkable treatment of women that permeates human history
and current society.

Similar pressures are at work in American culture as well,
though in more subtle and hidden ways. Women in the workplace, though they are often as gifted and qualified as men, have
not climbed the corporate ladder without a fight. Often there are
compromises to their femininity and basic dignity that are simply
seen as the price they must pay to make their way in the man's
world. They have left their children in daycare and tried to be

5   Dr. Emily Chong, *Women's Ministry in the Korean-American Presbyterian
    Church,* Doctoral dissertation, Fuller Theological Seminary, 2004; p.19

both male and female. Their marriages suffer, children are left home alone and the women are exhausted because they cannot do it all. The single woman thinks she will find peace and happiness if only she can find that perfect partner. Here is the ultimate irony: in all these efforts, they simply find themselves re-living the encounter with the enemy in Genesis 3—looking horizontally for the fulfillment that can only come from an intimate relationship with God the Father.

The woman's problem is that she is battling against a judgment pronounced upon her by God as a result of her sin, and there is no way to remove that judgment except in God's way. Today's woman, no matter how sophisticated and educated she may be, is still trapped in bondage to the opinions of others. She remains obsessed with gaining her identity and sense of security by what others think. And if by some mixture of personality strength, ability, and determination she has made her way in the world, she is still locked up in the prison of the opinions of those she considers to be important in her circles of relationship.

For the average woman the situation is much more basic. She is trapped in an unfulfilling marriage, frustrated with her husband because he does not seem to value her or understand her. As was stated earlier, the only way she knows how to connect with him is to try to become "one of the guys." Recently Marie and I were watching an interview on a Christian television broadcast. The hostess was interviewing a young couple who were having difficulties in their marriage. The wife made a comment that was revealing. She reported that in the early years of their marriage, their "dates" basically consisted of going to ballgames of various kinds. She was expected to fit into her husband's world, and there was no sense of interest or value for who she was or the things she cared about. Wanting to fit into his world, she simply remained quiet about her frustrations and needs. Many young women are waiting longer to get married out of the fear of being trapped in such a situation.

Many a wife who desires a spiritual orientation in her family is grieved that her husband is not more of a spiritual leader. She is convinced that if he would just get his life in order, everything would be all right for her and the family. So, she sets herself to improve him, determining that there are books that he should read, recordings that he should listen to, and conferences that he should attend in the hope that he will become a better role model in terms of prayer and spiritual guidance for the family. She uses her feminine wiles as a weapon, giving and withholding affection as it suits her strategies for getting what she wants.

Almost inevitably, instead of giving her what she hopes for, the husband becomes angry and frustrated, riddled with guilt over his own failure, and thoroughly tired of the pressure he feels from her. Instead of stepping up into his own destiny, he reacts against her nagging, often rising up and crushing her with anger and abuse, or punishing her with passive-aggressive withdrawal into his own world of self-fulfillment. A few days before Father's Day in 2007, I saw a TV advertisement on how women or children could help their dads develop their own "man-cave," a place of hibernation and retreat from the pressures of having to "be there" as the source for the family. While we recognize that each individual has legitimate needs for personal space and time, these behaviors are all too often about male self-indulgence, from relatively harmless pastimes such as sports or technology to the destructive world of pornography and illicit affairs.

The situation simply escalates from there. She either turns up the volume of her demands, or withdraws into *her* own fantasy world of media, work, shopping, eating, drinking, affairs—whatever it takes to soothe the pain of her heart.

At this time in our lives, Marie and I are among a lot of young people in their teens and twenties. So many of the young women share horror stories of the damaging experiences they have already suffered. Many are caught in the trap of food addictions and eating disorders such as bulimia and anorexia, needing the comfort of eating but then giving in to the pressures of body image. So they induce themselves to vomit, and then repeat the cycle, deepening their sense of shame and worthlessness.

Recently, Marie and I listened to the story of a fifteen-year-old girl describing her abusive relationship with her boyfriend. She told us that when he is angry he hits her and calls her terrible names. She stays in the relationship because she has come to believe two things: one, if she behaves well enough, he will love her; two, that something is terribly wrong with her, and therefore she is unlovable. To deal with her pain, she binges on food and then throws up. This behavior is epidemic among teen-age girls in our culture today.

The girl in our example was beset by toxic thought systems that were devastating to her physical, emotional, and spiritual health. In her fascinating book *"Who Switched Off My Brain?"* Dr. Caroline Leaf makes this most relevant observation:

Research shows that approximately 87% of illness can be attributed to our thought life, and approximately 13% to diet, genetics, and environment. Studies conclusively link more chronic diseases (also known as lifestyle diseases) to an epidemic of toxic emotions in our culture. ...The mind and body are integrally connected.[6]

6   Dr. Caroline Leaf, *Who Switched Off My Brain?*, Dr. Caroline Leaf, 2007. P.5

It is a desperate place to live. The woman's cry is simply this: *How will I ever escape this prison, and find out who I really am?*

Thanks be to God, there is a solution, and we will look at it soon. First, however, it's important to consider the judgment that came upon humanity because of the man and his part in this whole scenario.

CHAPTER THREE:

Eating The Fruit of Adam's Sin

On the other side of the gender line, the man finds himself cursed in similar ways. Although I am very careful not to de-emphasize the plight of women and the war that Satan is raging against them, the price that man has paid for Adam's sin is profound as well. Remember, *the enemy's attack against the woman was fundamentally an attack against the feminine side of human nature.* Whether we are male or female, the feminine side of our human makeup was given to us in order to hear the voice of God. The feminine, receptive dimension is an absolutely necessary component to effective manhood. *Without listening and receiving from God in humility, we men can never hope to stand in the masculine authority that we long for.* We were created to operate as Jesus did in relationship with His Father. As we hear the Father and respond to His voice, we are released into the place of authority and significance that is our destiny.

What About Adam's Responsibility?

Having said all that, we must also see the primary blame that needs to be laid at Adam's feet. He was the first to receive God's command, and he should have stepped in and stopped Eve's encounter with the serpent before it developed. Even after Eve ate the fruit, Adam's choices were not predetermined. Eve was deceived by the serpent, but Adam stepped into sin with full knowledge and with his eyes wide open. Therefore, God is absolutely just when He lays the blame for the sin of all mankind at the feet of Adam.[1]

Here is a fascinating question to meditate on. Though it is speculative, I believe that it warrants consideration. I wonder what would have happened if, when Eve ate the fruit, Adam had thrown himself before God in repentance and sorrow, taking the responsibility for the situation, covering his wife and pleading for her forgiveness. There are many records in the Bible of other leaders who repented on behalf of the people they were leading, even though they themselves were innocent of any wrongdoing.[2] If Adam, instead of eating the fruit and then blaming his wife, would have come before God in humility and stood in her place, perhaps something profound could have occurred. Perhaps God would have said something like this: *"Adam, the woman has sinned. She has done what I commanded must not be done, and now she must die."* And perhaps Adam would have responded by saying, *"But Father, I love her!"*

"So, Adam, I will create another woman for you."

*"But Father, I love **her**!"*

"Son, My Word is certain. The soul that sins must die."

"Then, Father, let me die in her place. Let her live. Give her another chance."

1   See Romans 5:12-17

2   See the examples of Moses in Exodus 32:32, of Ezra in Ezra 9, and of Paul in Romans 9. The ultimate example of course is Jesus' substitutionary death on the cross.

What if this conversation had taken place? I know it is speculative, and the point is moot, but in his still sinless condition, death would not have had a grip on Adam, and things could have been very different. We know this because ultimately Jesus did this very thing. On behalf of His Bride, because He was not willing that she would perish, Jesus offered Himself to the Father as the substitutionary sacrifice. Because He is sinless, death had no hold on Him, and in His life, death, and resurrection we now have the hope of being restored to the fullness of God's original intent for us.

Marie and I have a good friend who faced some of these issues in his relationship with his wife. Ken and JoAnn found themselves locked in the very situations that we've been writing about—JoAnn looking to Ken for affirmation and blessing, and Ken focusing on his work and ministry as the source of his identity and joy. Since both of them had come from broken marriages before they met and married, much pain was carried into the current relationship. Out of that pain, JoAnn found herself sinking into illness and depression, losing the battle with encroaching hopelessness.

At a certain point, Marie and I shared our thought processes with Ken, and urged him to change the focus of his life. Marie spoke particularly strongly to him, challenging him to lay down his ministry activities and focus on the well-being of his bride. Though it involved a difficult and complex process of disengaging, Ken took us seriously. He repented to the Lord for his habit of bending toward business meetings and ministry situations for his identity, and began to seek ways to give himself for his wife. As he did so, JoAnn began to believe that she was more important to him than his ministry opportunities. She also began to look to the Lord for her strength, rather than blaming Ken for his shortcomings. As this scenario unfolded over time, JoAnn began to recover from her physical issues, and they began to experience a renewal of romance and delight in their marriage.

Back to Adam. Instead of staying tuned to the Father's voice, Adam turned sideways to the voice of his wife, and heeded her counsel. The result was that he fell from his place of dominion, losing his ability to rule over the creation with the authority of his words. The curse that God spoke to him was this:

> *He told the Man: "Because you listened to your wife and ate from the tree that I commanded you not to eat from, 'Don't eat from this tree,' the very ground is cursed because of you; getting food from the ground will be as painful as having babies is for your wife; you'll be working in pain all your life long. The ground will sprout thorns and weeds, you'll get your food the hard way, planting and tilling and harvesting, sweating in the fields from dawn to dusk, until you return to that ground yourself, dead and buried; you started out as dirt, you'll end up dirt." (Genesis 3:17-19, The Message)*

Adam was created to stand alongside his wife under the authority of the Father's voice, and from that listening posture, speak to the creation and have it respond to his word. Jesus demonstrated this principle perfectly, because He only did what the Father was doing,[3] and only spoke what He heard from the Father.[4] Therefore, He had absolute authority and power on every word He uttered.[5] There was such life in Jesus' words, that even when He said things that were difficult to understand, His

3   See John 5:19-20

4   See John 8:28

5   See Luke 4:36

disciples stayed with Him. They realized that nobody else spoke words that made so much sense, and then demonstrated the power of those words in His interactions with people.[6]

By responding to Eve instead of obeying the clear direction he had from God, Adam relinquished the authority he had been given over the creation. It would no longer respond to his words; rather, he would have to battle the ground for his food, extracting by labor what he was intended to receive by blessing.

Let me illustrate what God intended this with a simple experience. It's an interesting story to tell here, because I'm going to use a woman to illustrate the point I want to make to men! Recently I was on my way to Kansas City from a ministry trip in Korea, and on the flight from San Francisco to Denver, the captain of the plane was a woman. I was pleased to see this, because over the last few years I've become more sensitized to the battle that women face to climb the ladder of success in our world. As she went through the checklist of things that a captain does on any normal flight, I noticed that her voice was calm and authoritative, and that there was no argument or resistance to her commands. The reason this was so had nothing to do with her gender, her personality, her looks, or her physical strength. The sole reason those around her listened to her words and obeyed them was because she had been granted authority through what she had received in her training. She had been instructed, had passed all the requirements, and was now operating under subordination to the rules of her job. Therefore, she was given the right to govern her aircraft. Because she had received her training and had cooperated with the process, she now had full authority to command and to expect her crew to follow her will. This woman understood authority and how it works—one listens and follows

6   See John 6:66-69; c.f. Psalm 45:2

the prescribed order of things, and therefore stands in complete authority and control.

By contrast, if I walked into the cockpit of the aircraft, and demanded to be allowed to fly the plane simply because I'm an individual male with rights and freedoms, I would not only be resisted, but probably arrested and put in jail! Authority only comes to those who *receive it* through embracing the process of qualification that is laid out by those in charge. This may irritate us, but the fact is, it's the way life works! The *longing* for authority and significance is normal in the human soul, but the freedom to actually exercise authority is only delegated to those who demonstrate that they are worthy to receive it.

It was the same in Jesus' life. Because Jesus never turned His face away from the Father, never tuned His ears to another voice, He was blessed with ultimate authority. He was able to speak blessing on a little portion of food, and watch it multiply to feed 5,000 men plus their families.[7] He had the authority to speak to a violent storm in the middle of a lake and watch it disappear.[8] He could walk on water as though it were concrete, and He could speak to sick people and see them healed, to demons and force them to submit to Him, and even to the dead and have them come back to life at the sound of His voice—every time, without fail. The key for us is to understand that Jesus did not do these things in the power of His divine nature; He did them as a man filled with the Holy Spirit, walking in the full authority that God meant for human beings to have.

This was the level of authority in which God intended Adam and Eve to walk. We know this is true, because under the command of Jesus' voice, the disciples did the same miracles that

7   See Luke 9:16
8   See Mark 4:39

He performed. What Jesus was doing was demonstrating normative human authority in the Kingdom of God, and showing His disciples that, if they continue in an intimate relationship with Him, listening to His voice alone and obeying Him, they could ask anything they desired and have it done for them as well!

As we stated before, if Adam had gone before the Lord to confess what had happened and ask for mercy and forgiveness, things might have turned out very differently, for God is good and merciful beyond our ability to comprehend. But by responding to Eve's voice (which at that point was under the control of the enemy), Adam forfeited this inheritance. Keil and Delitzsch's commentary on Genesis 3 is significant here:

> By listening to his wife, when deceived by the serpent, Adam had repudiated his superiority to the rest of creation. As a punishment, therefore, nature would henceforth offer resistance to his will. By breaking the divine command, he had set himself above his Maker, death would therefore show him the worthlessness of his own nature. *"Cursed is the ground for your sake; In toil you shall eat of it all the days of your life. Both thorns and thistles it shall bring forth for you, and you shall eat the herb of the field."* The curse pronounced on man's account upon the soil created for him, consisted in the fact that the earth no longer yielded spontaneously the fruits requisite for his maintenance, but the man was obliged to force out the necessaries of life by labor and strenuous exertion.[9]

Instead of speaking to the earth and watching it yield its in-

9   (from Keil & Delitzsch Commentary on the Old Testament: New Updated Edition, Electronic Database. Copyright (c) 1996 by Hendrickson Publishers, Inc.)

crease to him, he found himself having to extract things from the ground through sweaty labor. Instead of the creation being his servant, responding to his delegated authority that came by listening to the Father, Adam found himself in an adversarial posture with creation, having to wrestle with it for the very provision of his life.

Under the headline "Changing America," *USA Today* recently reported that more and more Americans are leaving their homes as early as 6 AM in order to complete their work. Therefore they have less time for relationship with friends and family. We men have to "wrestle with the ground" now, instead of speaking over it with the authority of godly blessing.

Furthermore, instead of receiving his identity and destiny from the Father, man finds himself looking horizontally for approval and recognition, just like the woman. *Her* diseased longing is for some man to tell her who she is, whether it be her earthly father, her husband, or a colleague at work. *His* diseased longing is for some man to validate him, whether it be his earthly father or his coach or his boss, or that he would be validated by the success of his ventures, or the sports team he cheers for, or the golf score he posted, or the size of his ministry. . . on and on and on.

The Tragic Dilemma Of Fallen Life

So both the man and the woman are now in a dilemma. They both know they need something from some authority outside themselves. God created them to pursue intimacy with Him so that He could give them the life of His kingdom on the earth. But now, because of their foolish and sinful choices, they are both looking for affirmation from sources that cannot give it to them. They are inevitably frustrated.

How does it play out? The man and woman go to work and try to extract from their work environment the sense of meaning and destiny that down inside they know they should have. But they cannot find it there, and so they constantly strive to find the right situation to meet their need. If it doesn't happen at work, then they look to other voices—recreation, ministry, or even illicit things like pornography or sexual affairs to try to find that affirmation. Or perhaps it's a situation where the woman stays home with the children, and feels reduced to being a baby-sitter, having no sense of adult communication or value.

The man in this situation comes home frustrated, only to find his equally frustrated wife waiting at the door with her list of what he needs to do to make her feel better. If only he were more spiritual, or a better father, or a more abundant provider, or if he were only at home more, or ... the list continues endlessly. When he finally can't take any more, he rises up in anger and shuts down the conversation or lashes out in verbal or physical violence. Or perhaps he simply withdraws into a non-communicative shell, leaving his wife more frustrated and lonely than ever. In the grip of his own frustration and rage, he strikes out against the woman, belittling her or abusing her, further destroying the feminine nature that gave him life. He also cuts himself off from his own ability to respond to God, which is his only hope for restoration. 1 Peter 3:7 instructs husbands in this way:

> *Give honor to your wives. Treat her with understanding as you live together. She may be weaker than you are, but she is your equal partner in God's gift of new life.* ***If you don't treat her as you should, your prayers will not be heard.*** *(NLT)*

When we mistreat our wives, God doesn't listen to our

prayers, and we can *never* reach our own potential!

When the husband is angry with his wife, he never considers the option of praying for her and listening to God to find the keys to unlock her heart. What he doesn't realize is that he will never reach his potential, never come to the destiny for which he was created until he can learn to honor her. As he learns this, he can then bless the feminine side of his own nature. This is what Paul means in Ephesians 5:28 when he declares that *"he who loves his wife loves himself."* Only in this way can he receive the affirmation from the Father's heart that will establish his own masculine identity. Part of this is that he must learn to love his wife and treat her like Jesus treats the people He loves. This process involves studying the life of Jesus in the Bible and seeing how He related to real human beings day after day in the real situations of life. As the man asks the Father for the power of the Holy Spirit to live like Jesus, the Father will begin to speak to him about how to love like Jesus loves. In fact, without this process the man will eventually come to hate his own distorted and stunted masculinity. True masculinity—exemplified by self-sacrificing love and tender, considerate authority—simply cannot surface without the healthy responsiveness of the feminine side of our personalities, listening to God for what He wants to say to us about loving our wives.

Let me see if I can illustrate my point through telling a story about some friends of ours who live in Seattle. Phil and Jeannie are true examples of a godly marriage, because Phil has made it his priority to see that Jeannie is fulfilled in her life. He is more interested in her success than in his, and it's amazing to watch the two of them relate to one another. Marie remembers one incident when a number of friends were traveling by boat to a certain spot where they were going to have a picnic. When they arrived at the destination, all the guys jumped off the boat to make things ready, but Phil waited for Jeannie, helping her off the boat and making sure she had what she needed. All through the day, he attended to her first, delighting in her, and showing her great affection. Though they were in their 50's at the time, and had been married over ten years, their romance was fresh and lively, and they became the envy of every couple there—at least all the women! Marie, who was single at the time, remembers telling the Lord that she wanted a DNA sample from Phil, because she wanted a husband just like him! The woman thrives under that kind of leadership, and her response is to honor and respect the man who uses his authority to honor and bless her.

Most working women, however, leave the work environment with their same basic needs unmet. A good friend of ours, who read the manuscript for this book and offered some very helpful suggestions, reported that he works with a group of women who express their needs with great force and volume, and who are quite willing to step on any person, male or female, that gets in the way of the achievement of their goals. Unfulfilled in her marketplace role, the contemporary professional woman often turns her focus to other endeavors. She's willing to try anything to satisfy the yearning in her soul to feel like she belongs, like she's more than just a worker bee in somebody else's hive. In her desperation, she uses her femininity to manipulate and control her situation, again attempting to exercise authority without the humility of listening.

The most common expression of this brokenness is the use of feminine sexuality—provocative clothing, or bartered affections—to generate feelings of power. If married, this woman is probably angry with her husband, and never considers praying over him, listening to God to discover how to exercise the true authority of speaking blessings as one who has heard them from the Holy Spirit. In her desperation, she raises her voice louder and louder, hoping to be heard and valued, but in fact only making those around her wish that she would be quiet.

Marie recently saw an interview with Hollywood personality Susan Sarandon, who is well-known for her strident feminism and overt sexuality. In this interview, Sarandon was questioned about an extremely revealing outfit she was wearing, and her response illustrated our point perfectly. She said that revealing her sexuality made her feel powerful, because she could sense the power that it gives her over men. What a tragic situation! This woman has completely missed what it means to be truly feminine, to receive power and authority from heaven, and to view her own body as holy, available only to her own husband as a vehicle of delight and ecstasy. As she ages and loses her physical attractiveness, her foolishness will become apparent, and she will be doomed to hopelessness and despair. This is not what God had in mind for her or for any woman. He has so much more for us if we will simply turn our hearts back to Him alone.

Single individuals are really in the same dilemma. They look for affirmation and identity from a variety of sources, when the original intention was to receive these things through an intimate friendship with God as Father and with Jesus as Bridegroom. The media in our day gleefully highlights the endless number of people who are locked in the desperate struggle of finding their identity and destiny. Even those we look to as heroes are tragically broken, and there really seems to be no hopeful answer. All we have to do is look at the headlines in the entertainment magazines, or watch CNN or Fox News to observe the glut of coverage of such tragic figures as Anna Nicole Smith or Britney Spears, or any number of other public icons. In our culture we crave heroes, someone we can idolize for a season, and then we watch in fascination and mock horror as they crash and burn in the futile search for significance. Somehow we find a morbid satisfaction that the rich and famous are also subject to the curse, and cannot find their way out of their dilemmas.

A Huge Complication

Here's a massive complicating factor in this whole matter: in a gross misunderstanding of Genesis 3:16, many religious voices over the years have insisted that this bent order is the divine order that God has for marriage. The teaching is usually brought in connection with the passages in Ephesians 5 and 1 Peter 3 that instruct the wife to submit to her husband. The unspoken assumption is that the husband has free reign to rule the roost however he chooses, and the godly wife is simply to be quiet and endure it.

The gross mistake is that very little if any responsibility is laid at the man's feet. These passages, which we will examine in a following chapter, actually put the larger burden upon the husband, commanding the man to love his wife *like Jesus loves the Church,* and to honor her and prefer her well-being over his own. However, most of us men are simply clueless about these commands. With little or no understanding of God's concept of love and of the way God intended life to be, husbands in every culture assume the authoritative role, and load the burden of submission on the backs of their wives. At the same time, they give very little thought to what God expects of them as they step into the place of leadership. The women are expected to submit to the husbands' whims, and simply bear up under the load, because after all, that command goes way back to Genesis 3.

Friends, nothing could be further from the truth! The woman was never intended to look to her earthly husband or to another person or to any other created entity for her identity and fulfillment. The husband was never meant to rule over the wife in a domineering and self-serving fashion; that's the way of the world's system. Jesus said in Mark 10:41-44 that leadership in God's way of doing things was not to be exercised by ruling, but by servanthood. God never intended the man to rule his wife by dominating her—that distortion happened as a result of the fall and the subsequent curse! And God never intended the man to be ruled by his bosses, or to exercise his authority over others in a domineering manner. Servanthood rooted in love is God's way, and we must become redeemed in our thinking in order to grasp it!

Marie and I recently rented a movie entitled *"A Good Year,"* starring Russell Crowe. It's a story about a very successful but heartless man named Max who is a big player in the London stock market. Max makes a lot of money, but treats his subordinates like animals, calling them "lab rats" and thinking nothing of using them for his own success. He also lives in fear of Sir Nigel, who is *his* boss. In one telling scene, Max is called in to Sir Nigel's office to give account for a particular action that was very bold and profitable, but very risky, and that got him and his firm into a lot of trouble. As Sir Nigel is rebuking him, Max interrupts to explain his actions. Sir Nigel spins around in fury and shouts in rage: *"Why are you talking? I'm not finished talking, so when I'm finished, then you can talk!"* It's a provoking and humiliating scene which illustrates the kind of leadership the world values, the kind that brings humiliation and destruction to anyone who gets in its way. It's a leadership style that perpetuates itself, descending down the food chain of corporate authority structures, and results in tremendous damage to the human soul, both to the victim and to the perpetrator.

Trapped in this environment, the average husband, wife, or single person finds themselves desperate and unfulfilled, angry at everything in general, and at their closest partners in particular. We take our frustration out on those closest to us, and then wonder why intimacy breaks down and marriages fail.

All this pain arises from the curse of sin and the judgment pronounced by God upon Adam and Eve in the Garden of Eden. It is impossible to overstate the devastation that has resulted from the foundational sin of the first humans. The spectrum of problems runs all the way from frustrated housewives in relatively benign situations to the overt and horrifying abuse of women that is so alarmingly common in our day. As I write this, the national news has been focused on the abduction of an 18-year-old girl from the parking lot of an upscale shopping center in Overland Park, Kansas. This girl came out of a department store in broad daylight, and was shoved into her car by an assailant that she did not see. She was missing for four days before being found strangled to death, her body abandoned in a shallow creek bed. Over 200 law enforcement officers followed every lead, trying to find the girl and at the same time attempting to track the young man whose image was captured on the video monitors in the parking lot of the shopping center. This individual was eventually arrested for the murder, with the facts of his own horrible childhood giving explanation for the rage and violence that exploded out of him. The daily news is filled with this kind of story, and the enemy of our souls rejoices to see one more young woman snuffed out before she could ever touch her destiny, and one more young man robbed by Satan of the destiny for which he was created by God.

Marie and I recently were in the prayer room at the International House of Prayer in Kansas City, where a young woman cried out in heart-felt prayer for mercy on those who are imprisoned in the sex trafficking trade that is rampant in our own nation. Some 50,000 women and children are held in literal slavery in the United States, owned, sold, and used in unconscionable ways to satisfy the lusts of the flesh. This curse is an incredible blight on the land, and stares us in the face as evidence that this nation that has known such blessing from the hand of God has turned against Him in drastic ways. In a current edition of the Kansas City Star, there was a report that twelve massage parlors, all located within a very prosperous county in the metropolitan Kansas City area, had been raided because of the suspicion of sex trafficking. In these parlors, a number of young Asian women had been imprisoned as prostitutes. They had little food, no clothing besides negligees, and were terrified in their captivity.[10] This is an abomination to the Lord, and the fact that it exists in our own back yard screams at us that justice must be done.

The next person who came to the microphone to intercede was a young father who repented in brokenness and weeping over the sins of his father's generation and his own for pursuing careers and self-fulfillment over the necessity of passing on the values of God's Kingdom to the coming generations. This self-centered agenda has resulted in massive addiction problems, the overwhelming statistics of abortion, divorce, and abuse at every level of relationship. It has resulted in the birth of an abandoned generation of youth who have no boundaries, no sense of moral absolutes, willing to do anything and everything that feels good in the moment. We teach our children that they are nothing but bits

10 The Kansas City Star, *Working To Help Women Trapped Behind The Veil,* by Lynn Franey, June 17, 2007

of protoplasm, evolved from animals, without spiritual moorings, and then we wonder and grieve when they act according to how we've trained them. We are astonished when the rage that accompanies feelings of insignificance boils up inside a young man and he takes weapons to an exclusive university and murders thirty-three fellow students and professors before killing himself. We as followers of Jesus are offended and shaken by these kinds of things, but to a great degree we must take responsibility for them because we have bought into the same value systems that give birth to such indecency. We have failed to exhibit what God had in mind, and to offer to the world the hope, the joy and peace of God's Kingdom as a viable and visible option.

These kinds of situations make us want to scream in anguish and rage at the insanity that grips our world. The results of the Genesis 3 catastrophe are obvious as we look at the disastrous realities of our culture. People are addicted to all sorts of lesser gods, and the fallout of abuse and dehumanizing behavior has become epidemic. Those who are believers in Jesus must come to see that we are living far below the norm that God had in mind for us. We must no longer be willing to live with things as they are. We must realize that we have been given the answers to these things in the Word of God, and by the power of the Holy Spirit we must declare that the Kingdom of God has come to set people free from these prisons. In the next chapter, we will examine the solution that is given to us in the Word of God for this dilemma.

CHAPTER FOUR:

Toward A Solution Of The Matter

*I*t's becoming really clear that looking to earthly, created sources for significance, identity, destiny, and fulfillment simply will not work because it is not what God intended for us. What He intended from the beginning was that we would want Him at the center of our lives, that we would love and worship God and His Son Jesus Christ with thankful and trusting hearts, and receive from Him all that we need for fulfillment. In turn, we would then display God's goodness to those around us, sharing all the good things that we have received from the Lord, trusting Him to continually replenish our resources. We must tune in to the true power of love as God defines it. As we do this, we will come to experience positive emotions such as appreciation, care, and compassion. As these emotions become more common to us, positive changes take place in our nervous system, our immune system, hormonal system, the brain and the heart. These things boost our health and longevity, and enable us to enjoy life as God intended.

So how does this work in the practical reality of modern life? The solution is not a new one, but it is one that has largely been ignored and untried by almost everyone. If you grew up in a religious setting, you have probably heard these words before, and there is a certain risk that you face as you proceed through this book. That risk is to assign the material to simply being a rehash of "the same ol' same ol'." The temptation then is to ignore what is being said, but that is dangerous. The individual who is chronically ill from a bad diet and no exercise hates it when the doctor prescribes a good diet and a renewed commitment to the despised workout regimen. But the fact is, a good diet and good exercise is the only way to good health, and like it or not, we must pay attention to and follow the good doctor's instructions if we want to live well. Therefore, I urge you to look at these things with new eyes, as though it is the first time you are encountering them. Approach them as you would approach a treasure hunt, and you will not be disappointed.

In October of 2007, the Chicago-area Willow Creek megachurch leaders made a radical and self-exposing declaration. Greg Hawkins, the executive pastor at Willow Creek, and Bill Hybels, the founding senior pastor, made public statements that their strategies of drawing people into participation in church programs did not result in the transformation of human lives into the character of Jesus Christ. Pastor Hybels said this:

> We made a mistake. What we should have done when people crossed the line of faith and become Christians, we should have started telling people and teaching people that they have to take responsibility to become 'self feeders.' We should have gotten people, taught people, how to read their Bible between services, how to do the spiritual practices much more aggressively on their own.[1]

1   Taken from "Willow Creek Repents?" the "Out Of Ur" blog, located at *blog.*

The simple fact is that there is no high-tech shortcut to spiritual depth and maturity in the character of Jesus. The main and plain things have to happen, and we must be willing to embrace the patterns that are laid out for us in the Bible.

If these ideas are new to you, let me assure you that you have an exhilarating journey ahead. The keys to being released from the grip of the curse are found in the principles that follow, and if you will embrace them and implement the suggestions, you will come to freedom over time. Success is guaranteed by the Spirit of God Himself, who spoke through the Apostle Paul and asserted that *"He who has begun a good work in you will complete it until the day of Jesus Christ." (Philippians 1:6)* It is wisdom for you to make every effort to embrace and apply the things that follow. These principles have worked for many throughout centuries of faithfulness to Jesus, and they will work for you as well, *but only if you actually do them!*

The central principle is found in Matthew 6:31-34, where Jesus speaks to us in a very direct way. We quoted this passage back in Chapter One, but read it in another translation:

> *Therefore do not worry, saying, "What shall we eat?' or "What shall we drink?' or 'What shall we wear?' For after all these things the Gentiles seek. For your heavenly Father knows that you need all these things. But seek first the kingdom of God and His righteousness, and all these things shall be added to you. Therefore do not worry about tomorrow, for tomorrow will worry about its own things. Each day has enough trouble of its own.[2] (NKJV)*

---

2   The last sentence is my paraphrase.

Because we have been so captured in the bent posture of the curse, we have looked at this passage with total unbelief that it could be real in our daily lives. We have assigned the truth of it to some future ideal time when Jesus is reigning on the earth, instead of understanding that Jesus desires to restore all things and give to us the benefits of the Kingdom of God now, in this life, even as we wait for the fullness of His Kingdom to be established when Jesus returns to the earth. So let me give some very practical steps to living in the reality of looking to God for everything related to our lives.

The First Step Is The Most Important One

So in a world that is so overwhelmingly broken, how do we begin to hope for some godly resolution? As we face the personal issues that flood over us day by day, how do we eliminate worry and move to the place of divine provision and blessing? The first step is to understand and believe that God desires to remove the curse from us, and that He has invited us into the same relationship of love with Him that Jesus has. While this sounds inconceivable to us, it is the precise focus of the prayers of Jesus in the last hours of His earthly life. By giving up His life for us, Jesus made this relationship with God possible. In John 17:20-23 Jesus prays these astonishing words to the Father:

> *I'm praying not only for them, but also for those who will believe in me because of them and their witness about me. **The goal is for all of them to become one heart and mind—just as you, Father, are in me and I in you, so they might be one heart and mind with us.** Then the world might believe that you, in fact, sent me. The same glory you gave me, I gave them, so they'll*

be as unified and together as we are—I in them and you in me. Then they'll be mature in this oneness, and give the godless world evidence that you've sent me and loved them in the same way you've loved me. (The Message)

The reason that God sent Jesus into the world in the first place was so that He might have a relationship of intimacy and partnership with you and me for all eternity. He came to forgive us for making the same choices that Adam and Eve made—rejecting God in our lives, choosing our own way, and looking in every other direction for what we can only receive from Him. Jesus came to live in this world as a man filled with the Holy Spirit so that He could re-establish relationship with God as the normal way to live. This is more than merely being saved from eternal separation and condemnation. This truth is about coming into the fullness of God's design, that we would be like Jesus, empowered by His Spirit to live like He lived on the earth in anticipation of His second coming.

Jesus came to be what the Bible calls "the Last Adam,"[3] to establish a new kind of human being. He made it possible to literally start over, to be "born again" in our spirits. This means we have hope to change our ways of thinking and acting, and that we can begin to live like God intended with His power filling and enabling us. All we need to do to begin the journey is to acknowledge that we, too, chose our own way and sinned against God.[4] By doing so, we deserved to be rejected by God and condemned.

But Jesus came to our rescue! Even though He was God, Jesus came to earth as a man, lived in perfect obedience to God His Father, and then took the responsibility of our sin upon Himself. He was punished instead of us, and died in our place. This was

3 See 1 Corinthians 15:45
4 See Isaiah 53:6

so that we could receive God's forgiveness and be restored to the kind of life for which God created us. As we confess to God that in our own way we did the same things Adam and Eve did, and ask Him for mercy, God is faithful to forgive us.[5] Then, when we acknowledge that Jesus has the right to be leader of our lives, and we give Him that right, wonderful things begin to happen. His plan is to give us a completely new start, to fill us with His own Spirit so that we might be able to know His love in a deeply personal way,[6] and begin to live in the intimacy and power that is ours by inheritance as followers of Jesus.

This is the essential first step, and there is no other way open, no other door by which we might come into the fullness God has for us.[7] Please hear this, and take it to heart for your own life, and for anyone with whom you have influence: there is no other way to know our identity, our destiny, and our place of significance apart from relationship with God through Jesus Christ. God designed us this way when He created us, and if we refuse to accept the path of discovery He has made available to us, we are doomed to fail sooner or later.

Trusting God for Personal Fulfillment

After this first step is taken, the next thing we can begin to do is to look to God the Father personally for our own sense of identity, destiny, and fulfillment. My thoughts concerning myself can only be accurate and healthy if they are based on God's thoughts concerning me. The question that most of us have is this: How do I get a clear sense of what God has for me?

---

5   See 1 John 1:9. It is also very important to acknowledge these things before other people who will help build a context of accountability and training.

6   See Ephesians 3:14-19

7   See John 14:6

One of the greatest examples in the Bible is that of Mary, the mother of Jesus. Mary was probably about fourteen years old when she had the most amazing and troubling encounter of her short life. The story is told in the first chapter of the Gospel of Luke how an angel, Gabriel, appeared before her and spoke a number of things that would change her life. The first thing Gabriel said to Mary was this: *"Rejoice, highly favored one, the Lord is with you; blessed are you among women."* Try to imagine being a young teenager and having that kind of experience! But here is the point: in God's mind, Mary was highly favored and blessed, and He desired to bless her with His presence! With that statement, Mary had a window into God's heart concerning her, and could begin to build her self-esteem based on His words.

The angel went on to calm Mary's fears, and then told her that as a virgin, she would conceive a child—Jesus—without ever having a sexual encounter with a man. She would give birth to this child who would be the Son of God, and who would become the Savior of the world and the King over all other kings. Now, there is a life vision for you! The encounter was overwhelming, the message unbelievable, and the implications staggering for her young life. She asked one question: *"How can this be, since I am a virgin?"* Gabriel told her that the power of God would come upon her, and, because nothing is impossible with God, this thing would happen. Finally, as an indicator that his words were true, Gabriel told Mary that her aged relative Elizabeth, who had been barren all her life, was also pregnant and would give birth to a son. Whenever Mary would question if that encounter was real, she could look at Elizabeth and be reassured. All Mary had to do was agree with what God said about her and the promise would come true.

Perhaps you might say that if an angel stood before you and

spoke to you, you could believe God's words as well! But here is the wonderful thing for all of us: we have a book called the Bible that is full of loving and affirming words from God to us. The Bible tells us much about what is in God's heart toward us, and with the help of the Holy Spirit, we can meditate on these things and form our self-image according to what God says. We can receive the power of the Holy Spirit, just as Mary did. Although we will not become pregnant as she did, we will receive the power to think, live, and act according to God's design. As this happens, we will be able to withstand the condemning and defeating messages that come toward us from other directions. In the two Appendices at the end of this book, we've given you some simple tools that you can use to begin this process of focusing on what God says about you.

Keys To Establishing Personal Security

John the Baptist was the child born to Mary's relative Elizabeth. As he grew into his manhood, he came to understand these truths perfectly, and the Gospel of John gives some of the keys to getting a grip on this kind of personal security:

> *John answered and said, "A man can receive nothing unless it has been given to him from heaven. You yourselves bear me witness, that I said, "I am not the Christ,' but, 'I have been sent before Him.' He who has the bride is the bridegroom; but the friend of the bridegroom, who stands and hears him, rejoices greatly because of the bridegroom's voice. Therefore this joy of mine is fulfilled. (John 3:27-29, NKJV)*

Just one comment before we look at the phrases in this passage: please understand that the statements here are true for all of God's children who believe what Jesus has done for them, male and female alike. Jesus has made a way for us to come to God on the basis of His life, death, and resurrection from the dead. When we accept the fact that He did it for us personally, He forgives us for any sins and failures in our lives, and invites us into His family. We are given the right to become children of God, not based on our human heritage, but based on the fact that God desires to have relationship with us.[8] There is absolutely no discrimination between men and women as we stand before God, and the Lord invites us all to come before Him with equal freedom. Paul the Apostle said it this way in his letter to the Christians in Galatia: *"There is neither Jew nor Greek, there is neither slave nor free, **there is neither male nor female;** for you are all one in Christ Jesus" (Galatians 3:28).* Because this is true, every one of us can apply these things to our lives without feeling excluded. So, as we look at the words of John the Baptist, please allow the Holy Spirit to impact your heart with what God wants you to see here.

The First Thing:
God Has Great Things For You To Receive

The first key in John's statement is to realize that God really does have a definitive plan concerning you, and has already made provision for all your needs. John said that *"a man can only receive what has been given to him from heaven."* This means that God has already established your identity, destiny, and provision from the beginning of time. The first thing for us not to do is to go out and strive to make something happen, because that is that old, bent activity of the curse. You see, there is nothing available to us except that which has been given from heaven. It's not that other things are inferior; there are no other things available. It

8   See John 1:12-13

is only an illusion to think that we can make a destiny of our own apart from God. Rather than striving to make a way for ourselves, we are invited to go into the Lord's presence and ask Him what He has for us.

Proverbs 25:2 tells us that it is God's glory to conceal a matter, but that it is the glory of kings to search out the matter. In other words, part of our dignity as those who have been given dominion over the earth is to search out the secrets of God's heart concerning His ways, so that we might implement His will on earth as it is in heaven. God will reveal His Kingdom to those who seek it first in the place of prayer, rather than trying to figure it out by striving. Prayer is not religious duty; it is the place to encounter our heavenly Father and receive revelation for all that we need and desire.

Marie, for example, loves to be creative and loves building projects. She knows that God formed her with a visionary and creative mind. So, some years ago when an idea came to her for developing a gourmet bagel restaurant, she became very excited. Marie began to pray over this thing, and God began to give her more ideas, and to put people in her path that would help her. She had instinctive "knowings" about the color scheme of the restaurant. Recipes and new food creations would pop into her head. When the restaurant first opened there were lines out the door because people loved the food and the atmosphere. God had created Marie for a destiny, and He loves to help us discover what He designed us for so that we will succeed. He loves to partner with us in the matters of our hearts, because He is our Father, and it is His delight to see us receive what He has for us.

One of the best ways to encounter God in prayer is by meditating on Jesus' interactions with people in the stories of the Gospels. Remember, Jesus came to do two things: He came to demonstrate what the Father is like, and He came to demonstrate what normal human existence is to be like. When we consider how Jesus related to the people around Him, we come to understand the character and personality of God our Father. As we learn to do this, we can enter into the same experiences through the use of our imaginations.[9] We can begin to feel what it was like to be touched by Jesus, to be loved by Him as He released the mercy of the Father to those He met. Through the life of Jesus, the Holy Spirit teaches us what the Father is like, how He relates to us, and how He speaks to us with that internal voice, awakening our hearts to know His love. It takes a little time to get used to praying in this way, but as you become familiar with the stories in the Gospels, you can begin to know the power of His love in your own experience.

Another way of interacting with God in prayer is to go to the Book of Psalms. Since there are 150 Psalms, I like to take about five of them per day, and make my way through the Psalms each month. My goal is not to get through the five Psalms, but rather to find one or two phrases that express what I'm feeling that day. It's helpful to see that the writers of the Psalms experienced the full range of situations that confront us as human beings, and they knew the heights and depths of emotional response. Therefore, their writings are easy to identify with.

When I find that one phrase that expresses my heart that day, I just say it—or even better, sing it—back to God over and over again, giving a voice to my feelings, and allowing the Holy Spirit to touch my heart with God's comfort. I'll read through the rest of that Psalm to discover how God answered the cry of that writer's heart, and then apply his answer to my situation. It's a great way to pray and to commune with my Father in heaven.

---

9   See Appendix A, *Praying Scripture "With the Mind in the Heart."*

These things are so very practical, and can help us with the real tensions that we encounter during the normal course of our lives. One friend, Angie, has several sisters with whom she has had a volatile relationship for many years. The sisters have a history of toxic, angry fights that would spontaneously explode seemingly from nowhere. One sister responds to the toxic atmosphere by becoming tough and impenetrable. Another sister responds by giving in to defeat, judging herself to be unlovable and unwanted. She spends her days filled with the fear of being left alone at the end of her life. Out of that fear, she creates situations that produce the very rejection she expects, and her fears are coming true. Angie, on the other hand, has turned to the Word of God to find freedom. She told us recently that one of these antagonistic situations had occurred, and she was burdened under the oppression of it. However, rather than giving in to the toxic thoughts, she turned to Psalm 6, and read these words:

O LORD, do not rebuke me in Your anger,
Nor chasten me in Your hot displeasure.
Have mercy on me, O LORD, for I am weak;
O LORD, heal me, for my bones are troubled.
My soul also is greatly troubled;
But You, O LORD—how long?
Return, O LORD, deliver me!
Oh, save me for Your mercies' sake!
For in death there is no remembrance of You;
In the grave who will give You thanks?
I am weary with my groaning;
All night I make my bed swim;
I drench my couch with my tears.
My eye wastes away because of grief;
It grows old because of all my enemies.

Depart from me, all you workers of iniquity;
For the LORD has heard the voice of my weeping.
The LORD has heard my supplication;
The LORD will receive my prayer.
Let all my enemies be ashamed and greatly troubled;
Let them turn back and be ashamed suddenly.

Angie began to pray these words, phrase by phrase, allowing herself to identify with the pain the writer was obviously feeling. Suddenly, she no longer felt alone in her fear, but felt that God was understanding her! By the time she got to the last four phrases, the anguish of her situation had lifted, and she experienced a new kind of freedom based on what God said about her. She did not try to become tough enough so that the pain didn't touch her. Neither did she give in to the negative things that were said. She found her strength in God's Word, and came to a place of freedom through it.

The best way to hear from the Father concerning your life is to meditate on the things He has to say about you in the Scriptures. I've attached an appendix with a number of key Bible verses that will speak to you about the Father's love for you.[10] A wonderful example of this specific kind of interaction with God happened to our granddaughter Brianna during a visit to the International House of Prayer in July of 2007. She came into our house one day after a session at the Summer Teen Intensive, and was all excited because she had received something from the Lord through studying the Song of Solomon. She had come across a verse in chapter two of the Song, where the King (who is a picture of Jesus) speaks to the Shulamite (who is a picture of God's people, the Bride of Christ) and says these words:

---

10   See Appendix B, *"Who I Am In Christ"*

Oh, my dove, in the clefts of the rock,
In the secret places of the cliff,
Let me see your face,
Let me hear your voice;
For your voice is sweet,
And your face is lovely.
(Song 2:14, NKJV)

Brianna was absolutely thrilled over this verse, because as she read it, something awoke in her heart, and she knew that Jesus was speaking those words to her in a deeply personal way. What a wonderful thing for a teen-aged girl to hear from the Lord! He gave her an anchor point of His own affections for her that will serve to stabilize her during the most tumultuous years of her life!

A friend named Krystal came along with Brianna to attend the Summer Teen Intensive. These girls are just beginning their relationship with Jesus, and so when they came home from a meeting one evening, we noticed that Krystal had a troubled expression. We asked what was going on, and she shared that during one of the prayer times, she had suddenly seen a vision of her mother in a hospital bed, surrounded by people. Since visions have not been part of Krystal's experience until now, we knew that she had experienced something real and startling. Krystal's mother has had health problems, and so she was understandably upset by the vision.

Marie and I explained to her that what was happening was a good thing. The vision did not mean that her mother was definitely going to get sick, but that God was revealing Satan's agenda to her so that she could pray for protection and healing. You see, God is able to simply do all these things on His own, but He desires to be partners with us in His activities, working with us as His children to experience the life and power of His Kingdom. As we prayed with Krystal, her mind and heart were settled, and she in fact felt excited that God would include her in His plans to protect and heal her mother. The next day, one of Krystal's leaders at the Teen Intensive was praying with her, and sensed that the Holy Spirit was going to partner with Krystal's prayers to bring healing to her mom! She was tremendously encouraged by this, and has found the strength to pray over her mom as a result. This is how things are supposed to work for all of us!

As we meet the Lord in the place of prayer, and come to know Him in the kindness and gentleness of His love for us, we begin to discover that He has wonderful things in store for us. We begin to rest in the confidence that our physical needs will be taken care of, and that God has planned encounters for us that will thrill our souls and establish us as His partners in the work of His kingdom. We will come to know what we have been given from heaven—an inheritance from our Father that no one can take away from us.

The Second Thing:
There is a God, and You are not Him

The second thing I want to point out from John the Baptist's statements is his claim *"I am not the Christ."* John declares that the people of God, whom he calls the Bride, belong to Jesus, and to no one else. Jesus' love for His people is so strong that the only language that is sufficient is to call Him the Bridegroom. John asserts that he is only the friend of the Bridegroom, and as such, his purpose is to serve the Bride of Christ, preparing her for Jesus' pleasure alone, making her ready for His return. He's like a combination of the best man and the maid of honor at a wedding. His job is to prepare things for the Bridegroom, to make everything ready, and to make the Bride as beautiful as possible so that the Bridegroom will be thrilled when He sees her.

In other words, the people who followed John did not exist for his fulfillment, or for the growth of his ministry. They had been entrusted to him so that he might prepare them for the pleasure of Jesus. He shows us that our relationships with people must be from a posture of serving them, not from the posture of extracting something from them. Under the curse, we demand something from others in order to get our own needs met, whether the need is pleasure, or security, or a sense of identity and destiny. Under the principles of God's Kingdom, we can selflessly serve those around us, knowing that our needs will be met by the Lord Himself. The people around us belong to Jesus, and we are to serve them as we would serve another Man's wife.

This principle is beautifully illustrated in the life of Jesus. The story is told in John chapter 13, where Jesus had prepared the Passover meal to eat with His disciples before He was crucified. At that encounter, Jesus washed the feet of His friends, modeling the humblest kind of servanthood, and showing His disciples how to express godly love to one another. But it is essential to see the secure place Jesus was standing in that gave Him the freedom to serve in such a way. Verses three and four of that chapter give us the information:

Jesus knew that the Father had put him in complete charge of everything, that he came from God and was on his way back to God. So he got up from the supper table, set aside his robe, and put on an apron. Then he poured water into a basin and began to wash the feet of the disciples, drying them with his apron. (The Message)

Jesus' humility and servanthood came from a confidence in what the Father had given Him from heaven. He had been put in charge *of everything!* He had come from God, and was on His way back to God; therefore, He could serve with absolute freedom and humility, not requiring anything from His followers, but simply giving Himself to them for the pleasure of the Father.

We have watched this principle at work in powerful ways in the International House of Prayer in Kansas City. There are literally hundreds of young adults who are worship leaders, singers, and musicians who make up the teams that fill a 24/7 schedule of intercessory worship at the IHOP-KC Missions Base. In the spring of 2007, IHOP-KC came into relationship with a world-wide television network called GOD TV, that catapulted the faces of our musicians and singers literally around the world. It has been amazing to watch how many of the mature singers and musicians have refused to allow the lure of television exposure to affect their lives. They continue to serve one another, not seeking the spotlight, but actually looking for more hidden places because the voice of Jesus and the presence of the Holy Spirit are more precious to them than worldly recognition. They don't need TV exposure to tell them who they are—they know who they are because Jesus speaks to them in the quiet place of hidden devotion.

As we become settled in the fact that God has established an inheritance for us, we can let go of the self-serving demands that we place on those around us, and simply serve them in such a way that they become beautiful for the Lord's pleasure.[11] This

---

11 I fully understand that great care must be taken if you find yourself in an abusive relationship with a spouse or another authority figure. Taking the role of a servant in humility is not the same as staying in an abusive relationship as a co-dependent. If you are in such a relationship, please seek professional help in how to deal with the situation in a positive and effective way.

is a challenge because this way is fundamentally opposed to the way the world's system works. In that system, you have to make your own way, take what is yours, and use the people around you to make sure you get what's coming to you.

But in the way of Jesus, you can trust Him and you can trust the Father to give you all that you need as you simply wait for His timing and will. Instead of focusing on what you need, you can give yourself away in kindness, serving others from a posture of freedom, rather than slavery or dependency. This is a great way to live! It is Jesus' way, and we were created to thrive in it.

The Third Thing:
Finding Joy Through Hearing Jesus' Voice

The third key from John's statements is that we understand that our personal joy comes to us through intimacy with Jesus, not primarily by doing something or gaining the approval of someone else. As a friend of the Bridegroom, John the Baptist focused on listening to the voice of the Lord Jesus. He heard the Bridegroom's voice, and his joy was made full. Our personal sense of joy and fulfillment is in hearing the voice of the Lord—defining us, speaking to us, fulfilling us in the arena of our personal needs. We declare that this is possible today, and essential if we are going to walk in the fullness of joy that God has for each of us. Again, this fullness of joy happens in the place of listening prayer, meditating on His Word in an unhurried fashion, waiting for Him to speak. If you want to know your identity, your significance to God, and your destiny in this world, you must take the time for the most important activity of your life.

Allen Hood, who is a friend and the Director of the Forerunner School of Ministry at the IHOP-Kansas City Missions Base, tells how he cultivated this ability to hear the Lord's voice for himself. In the early 1990's, the Holy Spirit captured Allen's heart with the message of God's love for him. So, in order to deepen his own understanding and experience of this, Allen bought a new Bible, and began to go through it, page by page. He underlined every phrase in that new Bible that speaks of God's love for His people. Then Allen took the time to pray over each phrase, meditating on it until the meaning of it connected with his heart. It took him two full years to finish that project, but it established in Allen's heart a deep understanding and experience of the love of God for him. He learned how to hear the Bridegroom's voice, and his joy became full.

Friends, this is how we were created to live. We were designed to thrive by hearing the voice of God, both as our Father and as our Bridegroom, telling us who we are, how much we are loved and cherished, and what He has for us as we walk with Him, work with Him, and trust in Him. If we neglect this most important activity, we will inevitably begin to demand that our needs be met by those around us, and our peace and confidence will begin to vanish like a mist in the wind.

In the next chapter, we're going to explore what it might look like to implement these thoughts into the real situations of life. Please read on!

CHAPTER FIVE:

Working It Out In Real Life

*I*n order for any principle to have real validity, we must be able to work it out in the context of the real-life situations that face us every day. If we cannot meaningfully apply principles we learn to the everyday realities of life, then they are not true and should be discarded. We believe that the things we are asserting in this book are not merely relevant to everyday life, but foundational to living successfully in our personal relationships, in our marriage and family relationships, and in the workplace.

In addition, if we are going to have credibility in teaching these things to others, we must develop a lifestyle that is congruent with the principles we are presenting. In other words, we have to practice what we preach in order for our words to have any lasting impact.

Marriage and family relationships provide the context in which these things are worked out at their most basic level. Instead of the cursed and bent posture of extracting our needs from each another and battling for the upper hand in relationships, there is to be the upright posture of listening, serving and blessing.

Our goal is to learn to hear the Word of the Lord concerning ourselves and those around us, especially our spouses and family members. The purpose of this "hearing" is not to control one another by spiritual manipulation, but to speak things from the Father's heart that will liberate the ones we love into the fullness of what God has for them. This means that when you're meditating in the Scriptures, you spend some time listening to what the Holy Spirit says about your spouse or your family members. Then when the Holy Spirit speaks something to you concerning them, you share it with your spouse and pray that the encouragement will strengthen and liberate them. It's like a refreshing spiritual shower in which we are made clean by what God says about us. In this way we help one another reach our full potential, without any flaws in our personalities or our behavior. Each of us is to stand in this role, listening to the Father's voice as He speaks concerning those we love, and those who are around us everyday. Instead of looking to them to meet our needs, we look to the Father and to the Bridegroom Jesus. Then we can bless the people around us in His Name, and make our goal to present one another to Jesus, fully pleasing and beautiful to Him when He returns.

We also must learn to listen to one another, honoring one another by giving full attention to what is being said by those we care about. Listening with full attention to your spouse and children is one of the key ways to communicate value and honor to them. Developing the art of listening can be a challenging task in this age of multi-tasking and media overload. We find that it is essential for us to turn off the TV and the computer, put aside the iPod, and give our full attention to each other frequently during the day, so that we might hear and understand what is going on in each another's heart.

I was personally impacted recently as I was reading a commentary on 1 Peter 3:7, in which the apostle urges husbands to honor their wives. As I studied that word "honor," I was impressed that part of the definition of the word meant "to delight in her conversation." Most of us husbands just simply don't do this, and I realized that I am guilty of this more often than I would like to admit! But if I'm going to honor my wife, and love her as Jesus loves His Bride, then I must purposefully cultivate the art of listening to her, just as Jesus listens to me when I pour out my heart about things that must seem so elementary to Him. His main goal is that I would realize He is fully present and available to me in our conversation. His purpose in listening to me is not to gain information, but to communicate value and love, giving His full attention to me as I pour out my heart to Him. In order to love my wife as Jesus loves me, I simply must learn to be really with her, to hear what she is expressing from her heart, and to delight in that as valuable and worthy of my full attention.

Husbands: You're the Key!

The primary responsibility for establishing this atmosphere in a home rests upon the husband/father. He has been given the role of leadership, but that role is not to be exercised with a tyrannical approach. Jesus leads by serving, by interceding over His Beloved night and day, hearing the Father's voice, understand His will and communicating it to the ones He loves.[1] Jesus models the tenderness and gentleness that He wants from His Bride and from those—both male and female—who exercise leadership among His people.[2] He listens to her, hears her cries, and understands the longings of her heart.[3] Husbands and lead-

1   See Romans 8:26-27, 34; also Hebrews 7:25

2   See Ezekiel 34:11-15

3   See Hebrews 4:15

ers, this is the kind of leadership you and I are to exercise—the kind that serves and blesses, that draws God's people into the fullness of what He has for them. We are the servants of another Man's wife—the Bride of Christ—and we must lead from that posture with a certain measure of fear and trembling, lest we bruise those that are precious to Him.

In the spring of 2007 I was asking the Holy Spirit to give me some help in praying over Marie. I asked some friends to help me pray for her, especially in the matters of protection and security as we seek to follow Jesus in a faithful way. One friend sent me the following prayer, which I now pray aloud over Marie every evening before we go to sleep. It's a beautiful prayer of blessing, and I encourage you husbands to use it or something like it to declare God's blessings over your wife. You'll be thrilled at the results! Here's the prayer:

Father God, in Jesus' amazing Name, we agree that Marie is an anointed intercessor, and that she is Your daughter and Your princess, and a Bride in preparation for her coming King. We decree that the past attacks and history are in the past. We declare that she is the head and not the tail, and that she is above and not beneath. We declare that Marie is blessed coming in and blessed going out. She is protected by the covenant of the blood of Jesus, by the fire of Your Holy Spirit, and by the angels You have ordained to be with her at all times.

We agree with Your plans for good, and we command all the angels to come that are rightly hers. We declare that Your presence is increasing in her spirit, and all around her, and all around our home. Marie is a living stone and is being set into Your house by Your hands according to the divine timetables of heaven. According to the prayer that Jesus taught us to pray, we cancel all evil, and we declare the enemy's plans to be null and void of any power or effect.

We thank You, Father, for fathering Marie and preparing her for such a time as this. In Jesus' amazing Name, Amen.

As I have made it a daily practice to speak this prayer over Marie, she has entered into a deeper place of trust and confidence in God, receiving these words as His words of blessing. If you husbands will do this with sincerity and regularity, God will do wonderful things in your wife!

As you grow in this listening mode, you will learn to recognize the Father's voice through many sources, although the Scriptures will always be the main channel of hearing. For example, Marie and I were watching a movie recently in which a young man spoke a very encouraging and liberating word to his girlfriend. He said to her, *"Why do you keep trying to fit in, when you were made to stand out?"* I immediately recognized the voice of the Holy Spirit speaking that phrase to me concerning Marie, and so I repeated it to her. It struck a deep chord in her heart, and so we have added that phrase to the prayer that I speak over her every night. It is our privilege and responsibility as priests, both male and female, to speak these things over our spouses, our family members, and any others that God has placed in our lives.

The second thing for husbands to remember is that God has given you this wife as a helper, suitable to your needs. This does not mean that she is your personal assistant, available to do all the tasks that you don't want to do. It means that she is your completion, the partner suitable to you, and that God specifically designed her to complete you and to help you. She is to be alongside you, tuning in to the spiritual realm, discerning danger that is coming your way, evaluating people and situations to help you determine the right decisions to make. Therefore, you must learn to listen to her, and take seriously the things she says. Without her input, a major part of your wisdom and discernment is missing, and you will find yourself in trouble sooner or later.

Remember, God Himself said that it was not good for the man to be alone. So, God created a helper suitable for the man. It is interesting to see that in John 14:26 Jesus refers to the Holy Spirit as "the Helper" that God sends to us to teach us all things and to remind us of all that Jesus says to us. A friend of mine who is a pastor in Knoxville, Tennessee told me that he had been meditating on this term "helper," and the Lord impressed him that the way he treated his wife was the way he would treat the Holy Spirit. If we husbands want the full blessing of God in our lives, we must learn to honor His voice that comes to us through our wives. By doing so, we not only get better wisdom for ourselves, but we lift them up to a higher place of dignity and honor. Believe me, it is in your best interest to honor your wife in this way. The Holy Spirit speaks to us husbands in 1 Peter 3:7 when He says this:

> . . .*You husbands must give honor to your wives. Treat her with understanding as you live together. She may be weaker than you are, **but she is your equal partner in God's gift of new life.** If you don't treat her as you should, your prayers will not be heard. (NLT, emphasis mine)*

Guys, we simply have to deal with what is being said here. We *must* give honor to our wives, because they are equal partners in what God has given to us! This honor involves treating her according to the value that is placed upon her. Since God deemed her worthy of the life of His Son, she is very valuable, and we must honor her according to God's value system. I recently received an email from a friend that reported to us that one of their pastors publicly referred to his wife as "the old heifer."[4] What a staggering and dishonoring statement that is! My first response was shock, and then fear as I prayed for this pastor to receive God's compassion and love for his wife before he experiences the jealousy of God over her.

There is a very sober warning at the end of that verse in 1 Peter 3—if you don't treat your wife rightly, God will not answer your prayers! Wow! The Lord considers your wife to be very important. He has entrusted her to you so that, in partnership with her, you both might be brought to the fullness of your destiny. Men, you cannot become what God created you to be without the completion that your wife brings. Unless God has given you the grace of true celibacy, and called you as an unmarried man to be complete in Him alone, you must realize that your wife is a joint-heir with you of the grace of life! Guys, that phrase "joint-heir" is only used four times in the New Testament, and the other three times it has to do with what we receive as our inheritance with Jesus when He returns to earth. Your wife is more important to you than you realize. If you do not recognize that and serve her as Jesus serves the ones He loves, you will not get what you want from God, no matter how pious and religious the rest of your life might seem to be.

---

4   For those readers who are not familiar with farm terms, a heifer is a female cow that has never given birth to a calf.

Wives: Your Part Is Very Important!

Wives, you are to stand in the role of being a suitable helper to your husbands. This is not a demeaning thing, but rather a place of great honor. You have been chosen by God to complement your husband, to be the perfect helper to stand with him as the Holy Spirit works God's will in his life. You have the privilege of hearing the voice of the Lord and bringing His counsel to your husband and family in the same way that the Holy Spirit brings the wisdom of God into a situation. If you will quiet yourselves, and listen to the voice of God, speaking what He says and resting in the confidence of His backing and support, you will find yourselves being lifted up into a place of honor and authority beyond what you thought was possible.

This has extensive implications for you wives, because if it is your desire to be taken seriously by your husband, then what you say needs to have the aroma of wisdom and godly counsel upon it. You can't just offer your opinions on things that matter; rather, let your opinions be formed by the influence of the Holy Spirit. Understand that if you wait on the Holy Spirit in prayer, He will give you wisdom concerning these things that will truly complete the understanding that God is giving your husband. Years ago, I was trying to get a grip on this principle in relationship with my first wife, Mary, who died of breast cancer in 2004. As I determined to listen better to her, she approached me one day to tell me that she realized if I was actually going to listen to her, then she needed to speak with godly wisdom, not just with her own off-the-top-of-her-head opinion.

I was the senior pastor of a Vineyard Church at the time, and Mary occasionally felt that decisions I was making were wrong—either not wise, or without a good sense of timing. I often would feel judged by her statements, and found them to be critical but not very helpful. As I set my heart to listen to her, she realized that her words needed to not be merely critical, but to have the wisdom of the Holy Spirit on them, to present real options and constructive alternatives to what I was choosing to do. She began to spend more time in prayer, getting a sense of what the Holy Spirit was speaking, and then sharing that information. It was a tremendously helpful change in our relationship.

The New Testament gives a powerful example of the kind of spirit that God honors among His daughters. The Apostle Peter writes to Godly women and says the following:

> *The same goes for you wives: Be good wives to your husbands, responsive to their needs. There are husbands who, indifferent as they are to any words about God, will be captivated by your life of holy beauty. What matters is not your outer appearance—the styling of your hair, the jewelry you wear, the cut of your clothes—but your inner disposition.*

> *Cultivate inner beauty, the gentle, gracious kind that God delights in. The holy women of old were beautiful before God that way, and were good, loyal wives to their husbands. Sarah, for instance, taking care of Abraham, would address him as "my dear husband." You'll be true daughters of Sarah if you do the same, unanxious and unintimidated. (1 Peter 3:1-6, The Message)*

I recognize that this paragraph is not politically correct in this age of gender-based abuse, women's rights and the feminist agenda. But we must insist that the Word of God is timeless, and that this kind of submission is consistent with how God sees life.

It's essential to see that the model for submission is not only Sarah, but Jesus Himself. In 1 Peter 2:21-25 it is Jesus who is the example of obedience and submission, and who was murdered by unsafe authority figures. Here's the catch: Jesus was ultimately safe because His trust was in the Father who loves Him perfectly! Because He trusted His Father's love and power, Jesus could risk living in a vulnerable relationship with weak people. The Father's trump card for His Son's murder was resurrection and an eternal existence at God's right hand.

Jesus' Father is also the perfect and righteous Judge who perfectly keeps track of every situation that you are in, and who will release righteous judgment in the perfect way in the perfect time for your life. Then, in 1 Peter 3 verse 1, the wives are called into that same trusting submission—not because their husbands are always trustworthy and wise, but because God is! Wives, in this calling to submission, you are especially invited into the life-style of Jesus Himself. In other words, you are invited to live in the same trusting relationship with Father God as your eternal Bridegroom, who is Jesus Himself! He did it first, so that you can have the assurance of His power and protection as you follow His example.

The same principles that govern the attitude and behavior of wives also speak to men and women who find themselves in subordinate positions in the marketplace. We realize that taking this posture requires that you be willing to risk taking a place of vulnerability. Because of what many of you have experienced, this can seem like a frightening proposition. But the promise is that Jesus has your best interests in the forefront of His mind; and that, if you and I will trust His love, He will work all things out for our benefit,[5] bringing perfect and absolute judgment at

---

5   See Romans 8:28

the end of the day.

This is not just theory. In the story that Peter is referencing, Abraham's wife Sarah twice found herself in a dangerous situation because her husband made foolish decisions based in his own fear. Because Sarah trusted God, He intervened, and threatened to kill some people if they didn't take care of her! God is really protective over His daughters who trust Him, and you can can trust Him to protect you as well.[6]

---

6 We understand that in this day there are many who find themselves in abusive and dangerous situations. We urge such people to find counsel and take steps to prevent future abuse. However, the principles we are teaching must be embraced at a heart level in order to move deeper into God's purposes.

CHAPTER SIX:

Will This Work In The Marketplace?

One of the most delightful experiences in life is to see these principles in action in work situations. What would happen if, instead of spending energy worrying about your provision, getting all stressed about whether the boss is paying enough attention to you, you began to believe Matthew 6:33—that if you make it your first priority to seek God's Kingdom, He will add everything else to you as well? I'm not talking about being lazy and irresponsible at work, and then saying, "Well, I'm just trusting God!" That is *not* what is in focus here.

Suppose you could go to work with a different mindset, one focused on establishing the Kingdom of God in the workplace. Instead of seeing yourself as the slave-laborer at the mercy of your boss-provider, you could approach the situation as a son or daughter of the Kingdom, sent by God into the situation to bring the influence and resources of God's reign. You would then see the boss and others around you as ones that God loves. You would understand that He wants so much to bless them that He sent you into the mix to establish a point of influence for the Kingdom of God. How would we live if we were confident that the Spirit of

God would interact with us concerning our work in such a way that blessing would come to us and through us every day?

Let me share a story with you of how the Holy Spirit broke into a workplace situation with wisdom from heaven for the success of one of His children. When Marie was launching her food business in the early 1980's, she had been given an idea from the Lord (although at the time it just seemed like a good idea from out of the blue). Marie was a new believer at the time, and the concept of hearing something from God was totally foreign to her. The idea was to insert a scoop of ice cream between two chocolate chip cookies, and make an ice cream sandwich. She experimented with the cookie dough recipes until she found a mix that would not turn soggy while in contact with the ice cream. Marie and her partner prepared a number of samples, put them in a plastic baggie, and without an appointment went to the corporate offices of Kemps-Marigold in Minneapolis to try to sell their idea.

Because God gave them favor, they were allowed to see the vice-president of the company, who loved the product and two weeks later gave them an order for three and one-half million cookies! Marie and her partner were understandably overwhelmed at the task that was suddenly before them.

As time went on, a facility had to be prepared for the mass production of the ice cream cookie sandwiches. Marie, who had zero experience in this sort of thing, was asked to come to the new plant and corporate offices to give input on the design of the machines that would prepare the sandwiches. As she journeyed to the site, she prayed a simple and childlike prayer for help in the situation. She and her partner met with the president who asked her what she thought about the design of the equipment to manufacture the product. When she walked into the production room, the production representative also asked Marie for her opinion on how this machinery should function. She immediately began to "see" with the eyes of her imagination, and began describing the design of the assembly line that would produce her product. When she finished, the engineer simply responded, "Yes, that will work!" and the idea became reality. Here's the point: the revelation from the Lord gave her authority in a situation where she would normally have had no influence whatever. In the midst of the workplace, the Holy Spirit, who is the divine Helper suitable to our needs, revealed what Marie could not know, and the blessing of the Lord came to her as a result.

Here's another story about this kind of marketplace intervention. I was having a conversation early in 2007 with my son-in-law, Ben, who is an accountant for a firm in Minneapolis that installs high-end sound systems for various companies. We were grilling hamburgers outside their home near the University of Minnesota when Ben told me that he was feeling somewhat disgruntled about his job. He felt that he was not being adequately compensated for his work, sensed that there was not a clear way open for his promotion, and was wondering if he had made the right decision in taking the position. A thought came into my mind that seemed to have some spiritual impact to it, so I shared it with him. I said something like this: "Ben, I'll make you a bet. Every time you start feeling disgruntled and impatient in your job, instead of complaining, turn that feeling into a time of prayer for your boss's success. Ask the Lord to bless the business, and to give favor to the boss at every level. Keep praying until that uneasy feeling disappears. And here's the bet—I'll bet you that your boss will come to you early, before the time for your annual review, and he'll offer you a raise and a promise of a better position in the future." Ben nodded, and agreed that he would do that, but frankly, I was not sure that he would follow through.

A few months later, I heard from my daughter Alyson that Ben was having his annual review, only it was happening three months before the year was up. A couple of days later I talked with Ben, and here's what happened: Ben took me up on my challenge, and for those few months, every time he felt discouraged or dissatisfied, Ben prayed for blessing on his boss and affirmed his own confidence in the Lord's provision. Then, Ben's boss came to him unexpectedly and said "I know it's early, but I'd like to do your review this week. We think you're a really good employee, and we want to keep you around, so come prepared to tell me what it will take to keep you here."

Ben was very surprised by this, and decided to push the envelope with his request for a raise. He chose what he thought was a substantial yearly increase, and brought that figure to the meeting. During the review, Ben's boss strongly affirmed Ben's role and importance to the company, and then he asked Ben about the financial issue. Ben laid it out for the boss, who acknowledged that it was a significant amount, more than he had expected Ben to ask for. He then *raised it* by over $2000 per year, and told Ben that he was being slated for a managerial position within the coming year. In addition, Ben was told that the raise would take effect immediately instead of at the normal end-of-the-year time. The whole situation was both a total shock and a blessing to Ben, and the fruit of seeking the Kingdom above his own interest was obvious. Ben was able to see that God really did respond to his prayers, and that he can therefore relax about his future and simply serve his boss with a good attitude to the best of his ability. The end result: everyone gets blessed in the process!

Could it be that this kind of thing should be the *norm* for believers in the workplace? Is there a group of people out there who will dare to live as though the Word of God is true and that He really means to keep the promises He made to us? It was a profound pleasure to listen to my daughter talk to her husband that night, telling him how proud she was of him, and blessing him for his Kingdom approach to this situation. How different this is from the average situation of fear, complaint, and accusation that brings destruction to so many situations.

What if husbands and wives were to take the same sort of approach to each other as Ben did to his boss? Instead of looking to each other as the source of security, provision and a sense of identity and blessing, they would look first to the Lord. They would listen to Him, meditating on the promises of His Word and trusting Him to actually do the things that He has promised. Then, instead of nagging and badgering each another, trying to extract from them what they cannot give, they would pray over each another, listening to the Father's voice to hear His thoughts concerning this precious person living in the same house. As they pray, they would sense the Father's pleasure over their spouse, and begin to speak the things that the Father is saying about them.

What would happen to your children if they saw these principles modeled in your lives? What if they knew that you were spending time in the presence of God, listening to Him speak about who they are in His understanding? What if they experienced the blessing of God as you speak to them about their lives and bless them in Jesus' name? How their hearts would resonate with the truth concerning them, and how they would rejoice as they were trained how to live according to God's design! There would be no need to worry about whether our daughters will dress too provocatively, or whether our sons will go to the internet for sexual stimulation. The protection of the Lord is promised to those who walk in righteousness, and to their children.[1] We would not have to worry about drugs or alcohol, because they would see in our lives and know from their own experience that fullness of joy is in the presence of the Lord, hearing His voice and receiving His Word.

As we learn how to hear the Father's voice, and set our hearts to follow Jesus alone, we will receive what He has to say to those around us, and through them, what He says to us. God is then free to use the voice of a leader, or of a spouse, or of a child to speak His Word. Since we're listening to the Father's voice, and to the Bridegroom's voice, and not looking for affirmation from horizontal sources, we can hear Him through His written Word, through the voice of the Holy Spirit, or through anyone He chooses as His spokesperson. Since He is the source of our provision, we can accept that provision through any channel He chooses. This is liberty! This is the way of the Kingdom. It's how Jesus lived, and it's how He desires for us to walk with Him and with each other as we wait for His coming.

In the final chapter, we will take one more look at the leadership style of Jesus, and how we can apply His principles of authority and submission to our lives.

---

1   Read Psalm 112 to gain insight into the blessings that are waiting for those who follow the plan of God for their lives.

CHAPTER SEVEN:

Authority and Submission in the Style of Jesus

As we come to the conclusion of this little volume, it is important to consider how to produce the right kind of headship and submission both in the Body of Christ and within the marriage relationship. Marie and I are clear that there is a God-given reality of order and mutual submission in Christian marriage. The issue here is not whether there is order, but whether we will remain stuck in the false and oppressive order that results from our fallen, bent posture. We want to look to the Holy Spirit to guide us into a right and truthful order that will bring liberty to the family of God.

One of the key passages in Scripture that comes into focus here is 1 Corinthians 11:3, which states that *"the head of every man is Christ, the head of woman is man, and the head of Christ is God."* This verse must be seen in harmony with verse seven of the same chapter, which says that man *"is the image and glory of God; but woman is the glory of man."* So, there is a role of headship by Christ and men that leads to glory for men and women. Let's examine these things a bit more closely together with what the Apostle Paul says in Ephesians 5:25-30—

*Husbands, go all out in your love for your wives, exactly
as Christ did for the church—a love marked by giving,
not getting. Christ's love makes the church whole. His
words evoke her beauty. Everything he does and says
is designed to bring the best out of her, dressing her in
dazzling white silk, radiant with holiness. And that is
how husbands ought to love their wives. They're really
doing themselves a favor—since they're already "one"
in marriage. No one abuses his own body, does he? No,
he feeds and pampers it. That's how Christ treats us, the
church, since we are part of his body. (The Message)*

These verses show us how Jesus loves His Bride, and therefore how we are to relate to one another in our marriages, our
families, and in the Body of Christ. Since we no longer need to
extract our significance from those around us, we can give ourselves for one another—husbands for your wives, wives for your
husbands, friends for friends.

Now, I'm not going to begin by speaking to wives about submitting to their husbands, or to everyday believers about submitting to their pastors and leaders. To address those issues first is
to put the cart before the horse. In order to understand headship within the context of marriage and/or Church leadership,
we must consider the nature of the headship that Jesus exercises
over the Church. In Ephesians 5:25 and following, we are given a
beautiful model for leadership authority that sets the context for
the issues of submission that face us. I am convinced that if we
followed the principles of Jesus' leadership that arise out of His
love for His Bride, we would have far fewer issues of brokenness
and separation in marriage, or conflict in matters of spiritual
leadership with the Body of Christ. Let's look at the style of Jesus
as the head of His Bride.

The Christ-like Leader Lays Down His Life For Others

Jesus gave Himself for the Church. There is a huge emphasis in our day on building large ministries and fulfilling visionary dreams and agendas at both the corporate and personal levels of the Church. Most leaders and husbands have lost the self-sacrificing element that is essential if we are to be Christ-like leaders. I'm not talking here about the sacrifice involved in tirelessly building the infrastructures of a business or of institutional Christianity. Nor am I talking about the sacrifices that are involved in being a success in one's personal field of endeavor. That kind of sacrifice often has negative implications for the ones around the leader/husband.[1] Such sacrifice can actually be self-serving in a wrong way, focusing on personal fulfillment or on the building of structures and programs rather than on relationships that build up people and equip them to fulfill their callings. Leadership styles that use people for the benefit of the leader and his vision are not rooted in the values of the Kingdom of God. Rather, they are rooted in the world's value system, a system that the Scripture calls "Babylon" and that is under judgment and will eventually be cast down, having been exposed as destructive and useless.[2]

The kind of self-sacrifice I'm speaking of is the selfless laying down of one's life *for the sake of the person who is loved.* Jesus came to His place of authority precisely because He sacrificed His own life that those He loved might come to salvation. He desired that those around Him would know the fullness of their identity and destiny in God's purposes. Jesus commanded us in

---

1   Again, whenever I speak of leaders, I am also speaking to women who find themselves in leadership roles, but who have adopted the world's model of what it means to be a leader.

2   See Revelation 14:8; 16:19; 17:5; 18:2, 10, 21

John 15:12 to love one another just as He loves us, and then in the very next verse He declares that the greatest kind of love is to lay down one's life for his friends. Beloved, this is more than simply dying for someone else. This means to give up our rights to our own short-term self-fulfillment so that those around us might come into their glory. Jesus sacrificed everything that was life-giving to Him—His position in heaven, His relationship with the Father, His dignity, His reputation, His right to be honored and worshipped—everything life-giving to Jesus was laid down for the sake of serving, redeeming, and glorifying the ones He loved. This is why the angels and saints in heaven sing this marvelous song about Jesus, the Lamb of God:

> *And they sang a new song:*
> *Worthy! Take the scroll, open its seals.*
> *Slain! Paying in blood, you bought men and women,*
> *Bought them back from all over the earth,*
> *Bought them back for God.*
> *Then you made them a Kingdom, Priests for our God,*
> *Priest-kings to rule over the earth.*
> *I looked again. I heard a company of Angels around the Throne, the Living Creatures, and the Elders—ten thousand times ten thousand their number, thousand after thousand after thousand in full song:*
> *The slain Lamb is worthy!*
> *Take the power, the wealth, the wisdom, the strength!*
> *Take the honor, the glory, the blessing!*
> *Then I heard every creature in Heaven and earth, in underworld and sea, join in, all voices in all places, singing:*
> *To the One on the Throne! To the Lamb!*
> *The blessing, the honor, the glory, the strength,*

For age after age after age.
The Four Living Creatures called out "Oh, Yes!" The
Elders fell to their knees and worshiped. (Revelation
5:9-14, The Message)

What this passage makes clear is that Jesus' pathway to honor and authority was one of self-sacrifice. It was *not* one of imposing His vision on those around Him and using them so that He could realize His destiny in the short term. Instead, He heard from the Father about those around Him and gave Himself sacrificially so that they could reach *their* potential. In most Christian marriages and in many Christian businesses or ministries that I've observed, the emphasis is not on laying down one's life for the Beloved, but in getting the Beloved—the individual's wife, the employees of the company, or the members of the congregation—to lay down their lives for the sake of the husband's career or the corporate vision of the business or ministry. Rather than making the Bride the focus of service, leaders are adopting the value of having low-maintenance Brides that don't get in the way of the vision being achieved. The emphasis is not on the leader or the husband laying down his life; it's on the Bride laying down her life for the sake of the career or the ministry vision. It seems pretty backwards to me! No wonder the wives or the employees or the church members struggle to survive and often have a difficult time submitting to the leaders!

The surprising reality is that, ultimately it really is in the leader's best interest to relate this way to those around him or her. Jesus understood that, in the dynamics of the Kingdom of God, the more glorious the people become, the more glory Jesus Himself receives! God's Word says in Ephesians 1:26 that His people are *"the fullness of Him (Jesus) who fills everything in everything."* In other words, Jesus understands that, for Him to receive all that is coming to Him from His Father, He must focus on bringing His people to *their* full potential. He is made full when we are made full.

Secondly, the priority of Jesus in Ephesians 5:26 is to wash and cleanse the Bride with the water of the Word of God. In other words, the priority of the husband/leader, second only to hearing the voice of the Bridegroom concerning himself, is to stand before the Lord to hear His word concerning the Bride, and to speak these words of blessing, identity, significance, and destiny over her until she comes into the fullness of *her* destiny. The first role of the husband/leader is to listen to the Father about the Bride, and then in a posture of great humility call her forward into the truth revealed from the Father's heart.

Where are the husbands, the business and Church leaders that labor in prayer over the identity and destiny of their wives and the people under their care? I don't see that happening much in marriages or in corporate structures. Again, much more energy is given to convincing the Bride to be a good team player, to promote the personal or corporate vision, and to give her resources to the successful realization of the family or the institution. She is called upon to sacrifice so that the husband/leader can fulfill his destiny. Beloved, this is not what I see in the Scriptures concerning Jesus' style of leadership.

In the third place, Ephesians 5:27 tells us that the highest priority of Jesus is that His Bride reach her full potential, that she grow into maturity free from spot or wrinkle, so that she might stand before her Beloved in the fullness of beauty and grace. Where are the husbands who would make the spiritual, psychological, and physical beauty of their wives their top priority? Where are the Church and business leaders who demonstrate that the maturity and fully expressed giftedness of their people is the priority of their time and energy?

Well, we say, this is simply not realistic in the world in which we live. The husband has to earn the income, and there simply has to be sacrifice on the part of the wife and family in order for him to ascend the corporate ladder. Oh, there is lip service paid to the idea that it's all done to provide for the family, but in the face of divorce statistics and demands for Christian counseling that statement rings pretty hollow. In fact, most of the striving up that proverbial ladder is not for the sake of the family, but for the purpose of personal recognition and identity. We as husbands and leaders do not generally spend ourselves for the purpose of presenting the Bride in all her glory and fulfillment. We have to a large degree bought into the secular value system, dictated by the spirit of the age, assuming that it is the only way life can work. We need to begin to ask this question: how do we exit that self-centered rat race and begin to exercise our leadership in the way that Jesus modeled it? How do we begin to be obedient to the commands of Ephesians 5 in our own marriages? What does it mean when it says that my priority as a husband in the image of Jesus is to make my wife glorious, and present her in the fullness of her beauty and destiny? Do I as a husband dare to believe that if I actually seek the Kingdom of God and His righteousness that God will really add everything else that I need?

I recently sat with a pastoral leader from another country who was giving me his assessment of the condition of pastoral leadership in his nation. He reported that most pastors are caught in a high-stress, task-oriented ministry style that emphasizes the growth of the institution. Their marriages have disintegrated because of neglect, to such a degree that many of the pastors and even many pastors' wives are turning to extramarital affairs to find some kind of companionship and release. This leader pleaded with Marie and me to come to their nation to model what it looks like for a man and a woman to stand side-by-side in ministry, preferring and honoring one another so that the Gospel of the Kingdom can once again have a credible witness to the world.

In the midst of what seems like a pretty bleak assessment of ordinary Church life, I was recently introduced to Larry Kreider, who is the leader of an emerging network of House Churches and cell-based congregations in the United States and around the world. As I listened to Larry talk about leadership and ministry, my heart was stirred and encouraged because he was using the same kind of language that the Holy Spirit is giving to us.

Within the Dove Christian Fellowship International network,[3] the highest priority for leaders is the mentoring, training, and releasing of men and women in their gifts of ministry for the building up of the Body of Christ, and not for the building of an institutional structure. Those with authority spend it on serving the ones they have been given, affirming their destiny, mentoring and releasing them into what God has given them. There are no barriers to function because of gender or race; rather, there is a focus on hearing from the Holy Spirit about the gifts and anointing that He has placed upon individuals, and then equipping and releasing them to do what they were created to do for the sake of building up the Body of Christ. These brothers and sisters are living out the principles of Ephesians 5 better than anyone else I've seen, and I praise God for their example.

Here again is the surprising thing. We as leaders and husbands will discover is that if we will operate in this way, we will find a greater degree of fulfillment in our own lives than we would have by operating in the old system. Remember, Paul said in Ephesians 5:28—*"He who loves his wife loves himself."* In other

3   Visit their website at *www.dcfi.org*

words, the way to real self-fulfillment is to learn to love our wives and give ourselves for them and for our people in the same way that Jesus did. Then we will experience the same result of full blessing that Jesus is anticipating from the Father as His people are brought to fullness when He returns to earth.

My suggestion is that if we husbands and leaders would begin to exercise our headship in Jesus' style, the issue of submission would cease being a problem for the wives, families, employees, and congregations. The thing that makes me want to follow Jesus is that I've become convinced that He has my best interests at heart, and that He will do everything in His power to make me glorious at the end of the day. As I become convinced of that, I will bow my knee to His leadership and gladly endure the process of glorification that He lays out for me. As I see His model of leadership, I gladly lay down my life for His purposes even as He has laid down His life for me. He has demonstrated His willingness to do everything it takes to make me glorious; how can I do less than anything He asks? And what He asks of me as a husband and leader is that I spend myself on learning how to make my wife glorious and help others around me find their greatness.

This is true headship, true leadership in the image of Christ. Perhaps it's time to begin to ask how we can walk this out in the crucible of our real relationships, and allow the chips to fall where they may with regard to the "success" of our careers or ministries. Who knows, maybe the Kingdom of God might come on the earth after all.

Exercising Authority Without Having A Position

Another issue that must be addressed is this: how do we as followers of Jesus function in the normal, subordinate roles that describe most of our lives from day to day? In the bent and broken posture of the curse, the world's way of defining authority, those who have positions of power—husbands, bosses, government leaders, law enforcement officers, religious leaders, parents, teachers—get to tell everybody else what to do. We believe that we have to have some sort of position of authority, some hierarchical role that allows us to assert our will in a given situation. We mistakenly assume that unless we are given a position of authority, we have no influence, we are without hope of fulfilling our destiny, and are therefore insignificant. We feel trapped in jobs, trapped in marriages, trapped in any number of situations in which we have little or no say in how things develop concerning ourselves, let alone any influence in the direction of the company or family we are involved in.

If we buy into that understanding of authority, we will rule tyrannically over our little sphere of influence in the same controlling, autocratic way. Or, if we find it impossible to assert ourselves in any overt way, we will find a way to manipulate the situations of our lives for our own benefit, using passive-aggressive behavior, the withholding of affection or cooperation for the purpose of getting our own way.

I believe that the Holy Spirit intends for us to learn how to exercise true authority in the same way that Jesus did when He was on the earth—as a servant with no institutional position. The authority that Jesus had came directly from His intimate relationship with His Father. He did not draw upon His divine nature as the God-man; rather, He purposely took the lowest possible place.[4] He was born in poverty to a couple from a town with a bad reputation.[5] He was assumed to be an illegitimate child be-

4   See Philippians 2:5-11
5   See John 1:46 where Nathanael asks if anything good can come from

cause no one besides those in His closest circle actually believed the conception story that Mary told.[6] He had no standing in the religious or political hierarchy of the day.[7] Jesus' only authority came from being with the Father, hearing His Word, and speaking and acting according to that Word. He related to those around Him under the direction of the Father, teaching them, healing them, and serving them with the love that fills the Father's heart. Jesus' words and deeds were the words and deeds of the Father; therefore He had the backing of the Father's power. Because of that dynamic, Jesus had great authority with those who received Him.

Here's the cool thing: you and I can do that. That's the greatest miracle of all! Through the life, death, and resurrection of Jesus and by the presence of the Holy Spirit in our hearts, we have been given the same relationship with the Father that Jesus enjoyed, and we can approach Him as His favorite sons and daughters. Let me say it again: we have been invited to cultivate a relationship of intimacy with God as our Father. Jesus promised in John 15 that as we become His friends—because we have intimate relationship with Him—He will make known to us everything the Father has shown Him.[8] To the degree that we listen and hear the Father's voice concerning our own lives and the lives of our families and others around us, we will begin to have influence as we speak His words. The human heart has been created to respond to the Father's voice, and when His word of encouragement, comfort, or exhortation comes through you, those

Nazareth.

6   See the blatant insult spoken to Jesus by the Pharisees in John 8:41—*"We were not born of fornication; we have one Father—God."*

7   These are the implications of Isaiah 53:2—*"He has no form or comeliness; and when we see Him, there is no beauty that we should desire Him."*

8   See John 15:15

who hear it will respond.

There is a powerful passage of Scripture found in Jeremiah 15 that speaks to this very issue:

The LORD replied, "If you return to me, I will restore you so you can continue to serve me. If you speak words that are worthy, you will be my spokesman. You are to influence them; do not let them influence you! They will fight against you like an attacking army, but I will make you as secure as a fortified wall. They will not conquer you, for I will protect and deliver you. I, the LORD, have spoken! Yes, I will certainly keep you safe from these wicked men. I will rescue you from their cruel hands." (Jeremiah 15:19-21 NLT)

God is speaking to Jeremiah, who is in the horrible position of being rejected by leaders as God's spokesman. He has no official place; all he has going for him is that the Word of the Lord has come to him. In that difficult place God tells Jeremiah that if he will turn to God alone, listening only to God's voice, then God will back him up, and give him protection and authority. If Jeremiah looks to God alone, and not to the approval of those around him, he will be God's own spokesman! God pledges to rescue Jeremiah from trouble, and to make him so strong that the resistance of the people will no longer affect him in a negative way. This is such a powerful word to us as we take our stand as people with no recognized authority.

Marie and I were recently in a conversation with our granddaughter, Brianna. An issue had confronted her in relation to a friend's behavior, and she took a stand that was righteous but unpopular among her peer group at school. A number of kids were speaking horrible things about her, and as she became aware of these attitudes, depression and anxiety began to creep into her mind and soul. So she came to us for help.

We began to pray over her, and to speak the Word of God over her from this passage in Jeremiah, from the book of Psalms, and from the Song Of Solomon. As we declared the truth of God's opinion, her depression began to lift, and Brianna came again into the liberty of being one of God's favorite children. She spent some personal quiet time meditating on these true things, and was set free.

From this reality comes our sense of significance and destiny. The Holy Spirit leads us into the situations that have been orchestrated for us by the Father in order that His love and power may be displayed.[9] As we go through our days, tuned in to the Father's voice, if we speak His words to those around us, we will begin to experience the wonder of being God's partners, the Father's sons and daughters who are the heirs of the family business. We will begin to see lives affected and changed, not because we lorded it over them, but because we served them in the power of the Spirit of God.

My wife Marie lives this kind of servant-life from day to day as well as anyone I know. Recently, she took a friend who is visiting from another country to see our chiropractor. As Marie was waiting for the appointment to conclude, she struck up a conversation with a young girl who was in the waiting room. It turned out that this girl had a horrible history of neglect and abuse. Her mother is a drug-addict, and from the time of her childhood Alisha has been required to tend her younger siblings, plus the children of other women while they did drugs and prostituted themselves for money. She was currently working two jobs and trying to finish high school so that she could go on to college and make

9   See Ephesians 2:10

a better life for herself. In the face of all this horror, Alisha has somehow determined that her life is going to be better than what she has experienced. Marie was able to listen to her, to pray with her, and to offer assistance to her in some simple but meaningful ways, and this young girl was encouraged and strengthened by the encounter. This is the kind of ministry Jesus did, and the Father has all sorts of encounters prepared for you and me if we will simply listen to His voice and obey it.

As we live this way from day to day, the Father is free to bring to us more and more people, more and more situations that we can touch with His power, and we begin to discover who we truly are.

With all our hearts we urge you to put these things to the test in your own life. There is a way to escape the penalty of the curse of sin, and you can begin to experience it today.

The Conclusion Of The Matter

So, the great question that faces us as we come to the end of this little study is this: are there some practical ways to work these things out in the reality of our day-to-day lives? Is there some formula for success, some prescribed routine or solution that will help us extract ourselves from the old bent and broken way and begin a new life of freedom?

The good news is that Jesus has invited us to follow Him in this adventure by the leading of the Holy Spirit. Therefore, He has not given us a formula; rather, He has demonstrated in His own life what it means to walk in a day-by-day relationship with the Father through the Holy Spirit. This must be cultivated in the heart of every individual, coming to Him each day as you would to a friend who desires to walk alongside you step by step.

Our advice to you is this: read the Gospels over and over. Think through the encounters that Jesus had with people, and use your imagination to sense and feel the leading of the Spirit in His life as He saw and did what the Father was doing. This is about an intimate relationship with Jesus as the leader and model for our lives. Each one of us has to work this out in the context of his own life.

The first step is really the most difficult. It involves admitting that the old way simply doesn't work, and becoming willing to renounce the way we have approached life up to now. It involves a willingness to venture out into something new and unfamiliar, a desire to experience a new kind of living that is strong enough to overcome our addiction to the familiar but broken ways we have lived until now.

I trust you will find the courage to take this first step. Call upon the Lord, and He will lead you. The Holy Spirit will be your escort into this new way of living.

Father, we pray now over each person who reads this book, and who sets their heart and mind to pursue You in this way. Send Your Holy Spirit as the escort in this process. Release the Spirit of wisdom and revelation to them, and cause them to know the depths of Your love and delight in them. Show them the wonderful things You have prepared for them, and grant them the grace to walk this out day by day, trusting You for the fullness of their joy and peace. In Jesus' Name we ask these things. Amen.

Praying Scripture with the 'Mind in the Heart'

1. Entering In – Becoming Aware of His Loving Presence

Remembering that the eye of the Lord is constantly watching over those who revere and love Him, still yourself and become aware of God. Welcome and settle into His presence, which actually already enfolds you. As you become present to Him and His loving gaze, what do you sense, what do you see in His eyes? Linger attentively and receptively for several moments, asking God to help you see what is in His heart toward you as you turn the eyes of your heart to meet His loving gaze with yours.

2. Pray for His Grace

Ask God in faith for a particular aspect of His grace, e.g., for your mind to be touched and opened, to be enabled to see the invisible, to hear the inaudible, to fathom the unfathomable, to perceive the intangible, for your heart to be good ground for the seed of God's Word, for the grace to know Him more intimately, to desire and love Him more purely, etc.

3. Scripture Meditation

It is essential that, while we hold to the Word of God as being God-breathed, we realize that the Scriptures are to actually lead us *beyond the written words* to an *encounter with the living, Eternal Word*. Jesus said to the Jews (John 5:39-40), *'You search the Scriptures, because you think that in them you have eternal life; and it is these that point to/lead you to Me; and you are unwilling to come **to Me, that you may have life.'*** These Jews were diligent to study, search the Scriptures minutely, and were full of the head-knowledge of holy words. But they had not gone *through and beyond* the Word of God, to The God-Word Himself. Consequently, though they were 'full of the Word' in terms of written Scripture, *they had no life in themselves.* In this sense, we need to view Scripture as a 'window' into and through which we gaze intently until we 'behold the Word'—until we see, hear, sense, know the Lord encountering us personally, deep on the inside. It is in the infinite depths of our souls, our innermost beings, far beyond the mere entryway of our minds, where God reaches to touch us with His Word, to woo us in love, to profoundly and continually convert and transform us until we are formed into the image and likeness of the Lord Jesus whom we are beholding (2 Cor 3:18).

Our goal, then, is to pray with Scripture in such a way that the holy words which enter our minds permeate deeper, leading to holy encounter within our hearts. The early Church Fathers described this way of coming to God as 'praying with the mind in the heart,' 'bringing the mind into the heart,' or simply as 'the prayer of the heart.' There are three phases involved in this way of praying with Scripture with our minds in our hearts.

a. **Meditation.** Read your selected passage repeatedly, very slowly in a relaxed but alert manner. It may be helpful to read from a couple of versions, being careful however not to become 'busy' or distracted with comparing texts and studying, as the mode of reading and praying here is biblical meditation. Meditation makes space for God to *encounter and connect* with us through the Word. If you are reading a parable or event in the Gospels, it is especially helpful to 'enter' the story by imagining you are one of the characters. *You* become the blind beggar, the prodigal son, the fisherman being called to follow Jesus, etc. Read slowly, prayerfully, attentively until a word or words, a phrase, a thought speaks to you, inviting you to pause and ponder more deeply. Allow questions to form, new thoughts and insights to emerge and unfold. When you sense that 'connection,' that what you are reading is somehow touching your mind and heart, respond to that invitation to pause. Your thought may seem like the tiniest kernel, but stop and stay with that word, phrase or thought, allowing your prayer to deepen into a closer encounter between God and yourself.

b. **Contemplation: A Meeting of Hearts Human and Divine.** This is the phase in prayer when we give unhurried space to the ministry of the Holy Spirit, allowing Him to take the 'kernel' we've received in our meditation, and unfold it within us more fully. The Spirit of God brings the Word from the mind down into the heart, where it begins to have a powerful affect. The living Word saturates the heart, melting and transforming it, evoking within and from it a deep, profound response of love, devotion, abandon and conformity to God and His will. As the Holy Spirit works in this way, we become aware that rather than simply reading the Word, we are absorbing it at a deep level. Truth—Christ Himself—is penetrating our inmost parts, actively working within us. The Eternal Word comes in love to actively fill, possess, and transform our souls. He kindles the core of our being into a flame of love and devotion for God, joining our spirit to God's in this prayer of true, holy communion. (1 Cor 6:17).

Surely this was something of what Augustine of Hippo was savoring in God when he penned these words in prayer: *"... Your Word touched my heart, and I began to love You..."*

When this contemplative phase of dynamic, illuminative prayer recedes, then simply enjoy the love of God and allow time for resting in and with Him.

c. **Mutual Rest** is staying with God in His presence, resting in His love and being aware that He too is resting in yours. During this time of sweet interior communion with God, simply rest—be—in Him. Just rest, drinking in His life, peace, joy and strength, allowing His Spirit to fill you anew. Rest in and with God, in the awareness that the Holy Spirit is brooding and hovering over you. He is watching over His Word to fulfill it, establishing and deeply implanting what the Father has sown in your spirit during your time of prayer and Scripture meditation.

4. Response

St. Ignatius strongly encourages us to seal our time of prayer by recording a concise, three-fold response in a prayer journal.

a. **'Kernel summary.'** What are the significant kernels I want to keep with me? What has God *said* to or *done inside* me as I've been with Him?

b. **Personal application.** What *response, change, or step of obedience* has God prompted in me in during this prayer time? Is there a step of action I need to take? Righting a wrong, reconciling a damaged relationship, following through on something God wants me to do, say, or become?

c. **Write a simple prayer** of response to God. You may find it helpful and enriching to write a brief prayer to each person of the Trinity, reflecting the different facets and ministries of God revealed in Father, Son and Holy Spirit.

5. Take-Away

From this time of focused prayer and meditation, carry your **kernel** and your *heart response into your day.* These become bread for the day's journey, to be brought out often for further chewing, savoring, and digesting throughout the day's work and activities. Then at day's end, it is wonderful to drift off to sleep with our hearts and minds still praying -- pondering, treasuring and delighting in God and His Word.

This prayer pattern can be used very meaningfully and fruitfully within a time frame of half-hour to an hour.

APPENDIX B:

"Who I Am In Christ"

Lord, I declare the following Scriptures over my life so that I know without a doubt who I am in You:

1. I am now God's child – 1 John 3:2
2. I am born of the imperishable seed of God's Word – 1 Peter 1:23
3. I am loved by Christ and freed from my sins – Revelation 1:5
4. I am forgiven of all my sins – Ephesians 1:7
5. I am justified from all things – Acts 13:39
6. I am the righteousness of God in Christ – 2 Corinthians 5:21
7. I am free from all condemnation – Romans 8:1
8. I can forget the past – Philippians 3:13
9. I am reconciled to God – 2 Corinthians 5:18
10. I am beloved of God – 1 John 4:10
11. I am a saint and loved by God – Romans 1:7
12. I am holy and without blame before Him – Ephesians 1:4
13. I am the head and not the tail – Deuteronomy 28:13

14. I am called of God by the grace given in Christ – 1 Timothy 1:9

15. I am brought near by the blood of Christ – Ephesians 2:13

16. I have been given fullness in Christ – Colossians 2:10

17. I am delivered from the power of darkness – Colossians 1:13

18. I am an ambassador for Christ – 2 Corinthians 5:20

19. I am the salt of the earth – Matthew 5:13

20. I am the light of the world – Matthew 5:14

21. I am dead to sin – Romans 6:2

22. I am alive to God – Romans 6:11

23. I am raised up with Christ and seated in heavenly realms – Ephesians 2:6

24. I am a king and a priest to God – Revelation 1:6

25. I am loved with an everlasting love – Jeremiah 31:3

26. I am an heir of God and a joint heir with Christ – Romans 8:17

27. I am qualified to share in the inheritance of the kingdom – Colossians 1:12

28. I am more than a conqueror – Romans 8:37

29. I am healed by the wounds of Jesus – 1 Peter 2:24

30. I am built on the foundations of the apostles and prophets, with Jesus Christ Himself as the chief cornerstone – Ephesians 2:20

31. I am in Christ Jesus by God's act – 1 Corinthians 1:30

32. I am kept by God's power – 1 Peter 1:5

33. I am sealed with the promised Holy Spirit – Ephesians 1:13

34. I have everlasting life – John 5:24

35. I am crucified with Christ nevertheless I live – Galatians 2:20

36. I am a partaker of the divine nature – 2 Peter 1:4

37. I have been given all things that pertain to life and godliness – 2 Peter 1:3

38. I have been blessed with every spiritual blessing in Christ – Ephesians 1:3

39. I have peace with God – Romans 5:1

40. I am a chosen royal priest – 1 Peter 2:9

41. I can do all things through Christ who strengthens me – Philippians 4:13

42. I have all my needs met by God according to His riches in glory in Christ Jesus – Philippians 4:19

43. I shall do even greater works than Jesus did – John 14:12

44. I am being kept strong and blameless to the end – 1 Corinthians 1:8

45. I am chosen by Him – 1 Thessalonians 1:4

46. I overcome the world – 1 John 5:4

47. I have a guaranteed inheritance – Ephesians 1:14

48. I am a fellow citizen in God's household – Ephesians 2:19

49. Christ's truth has set me free – John 8:32

50. I always triumph in Christ – 2 Corinthians 2:14

51. I am in Jesus Christ's hands – John 10:28

52. I am holy, without blemish, and free from accusation – Colossians 1:22

53. Christ in me is my hope of glory – Colossians 1:27

54. I am anointed by the Holy One – 1 John 2:20

55. God's love is lavished on me – 1 John 3:1

56. He is able to keep me from falling and to present me without fault – Jude 24

57. I am God's House – Hebrews 3:6

58. God has given me a spirit of power, of love, and of self-discipline – 2 Timothy 1:7

59. I am convinced that He is able to guard what I have entrusted to Him – 2 Timothy 1:12

60. He has considered me faithful and appointed me to His service – 1 Timothy 1:12

61. I am justified by faith – Romans 3:28

62. The Spirit Himself intercedes for me – Romans 8:26

63. Inwardly I am being renewed day by day – 2 Corinthians 4:16

64. It is for freedom that Christ has set me free – Galatians 5:1

65. I am held together by Him – Colossians 1:17

66. I have the mind of Christ – 1 Corinthians 2:16

© Called Together, Steve and Mary Prokopchak, (Lititz, PA: House To House Publications, 2003).